store
DESIGN

store DESIGN

A Complete Guide to Designing Successful Retail Stores

William R. Green

A
Zippy Books
Paper-Bound
112-901-609

ISBN-13:   978-0615676395 (Zippy Books)
ISBN-10:   0615676391
Back Cover "Storefront" image: © Giorgio Fochesato

Author: William R. Green

Visit My Author Page: www.wgreen.me

CONTENTS

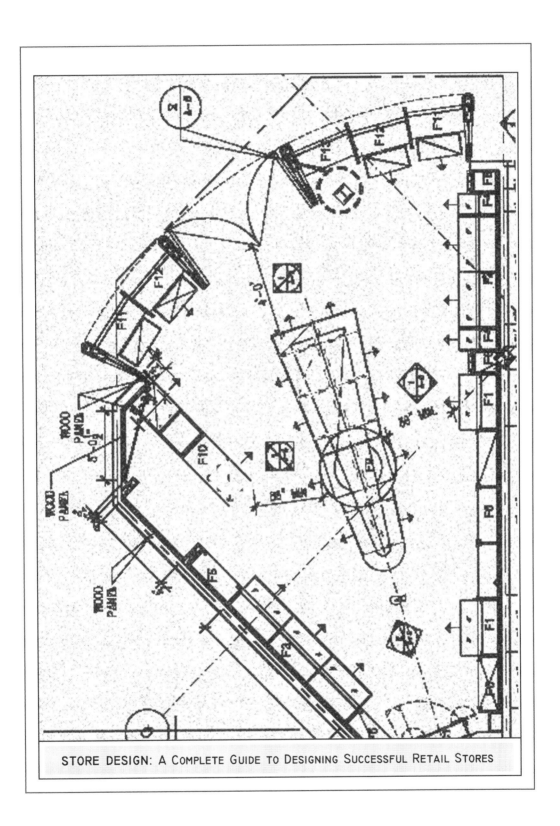

STORE DESIGN: A COMPLETE GUIDE TO DESIGNING SUCCESSFUL RETAIL STORES

INTRODUCTION

Why design retail stores? For many years, this corner of the built-world was considered a bargain basement by the public as well as by architects and other designers. But over the past few decades, retail designing has achieved public and industry recognition, acclaim, and respect. New store facades have pushed the limits of enclosure technology and high-design stores like those for *Apple*, *Nike* and others have been elevated to museum-like status. Internationally, thousands of *Starbucks* stores have become "the third place" between home and work—a place to meet, greet and be in public. Retail is not just about selling products; it is also an important social connector between the digital and analog worlds—between the intangible and the tangible. Stores and the social interactions they facilitate are significant *places* for people. Society seems to be recognizing this fact and the quality of retail design is constantly improving while its programmatic requirements are always changing to meet society's needs. In sum, the business of retail store design is now more exciting, and more relevant than ever.

Retail stores are usually fast track projects. A modest-sized store may have a timetable of 16–24 weeks from the signing of the owner design agreement to the grand opening. These compressed design/construction timetables guarantee that the designer will never become bored with a project. In fact, they create their own excitement. They move so quickly that the actual construction of a prototype sometimes takes the place of the presentation and modeling modes typical in the design of other building types. Therefore, the fruits of design labor are very quickly visible. This compressed timeframe is fitting for the age we live, and makes stores a good project type for those who are accustomed to moving in a quick-paced digital world, and who might find the longer duration of other project types difficult. The speed of store projects is exhilarating.

Some store designs, namely boutiques, offer the opportunity to build with budgets not found in other building types. It is not unusual for small stores to include materials, details and lighting otherwise found only in the design of corporate boardrooms, luxury residential units and high-tech facilities. Designers love to spend other people's money (wisely of course), and the design of boutique stores can provide this opportunity. There is no room for waste in today's downsized and efficient stores. This requires the designer be a crafty crafter.

Store design often incorporates state of the art technology. Sometimes it provides a retailer an edge over its competition or creates new ways to display merchandise, complete transactions, or tell the product story…think of all the special glazing details which have been developed for storefronts; the computerized electronics to process sales transactions; state of the art lighting techniques (LED, fiber optics, projector lighting); the early use of multiple screen and flat screen technology; the mechanical introduction of mind-altering smells to induce shopper purchases; and the use of music, sounds, and colors to induce other desired patterns of shopper behavior. The careful selection of lighting and materials to create environmentally conscious "green" stores that function well and meet or better their retail competitors is a challenge that designers welcome.

Store designers can have as much fun as movie-set, and computer game designers by creating an imaginary world, which would not have existed, but for the designer. They often break through conventions quickly creating new design trends. Thus store designers "live on the edge". Dealing in this bold, highly competitive, fast-paced environment, has many rewards. It is exciting, and challenging. It has roots in the theatrical arts and stage design. Like the constructed elements of a theatrical production, executed store designs rely on dramatic lighting, effective visual presentation, and knowledge of human psychology. Retailing is an ever-changing business responding always to market forces, technology and the development new retail concepts. At present, electronic retailing is having a dramatic effect on physical store retailing and in some cases has eliminated retail concepts that only a few years ago were "the next big thing". So it goes in this industry.

Therefore, the store designer must be able to react quickly to changing trends and possess a kit of design tools that will be just as sharp and useful in the decades to come as today. *Store Design* was created with that goal in mind. It utilizes axiomatic design principles that may be understood and implemented to create successful retail stores, restaurants, showrooms or any other space having similar programmatic requirements. The design concepts presented in this book are simple, but effective.

As *Nike* says: "*Just Do It!*" Have fun, imagine, and create.

CHAPTER 1 --- IMAGE

The importance of store image is best exemplified by comparing a store to a movie. The customer visiting a store or a movie theater has certain expectations. If the movie is a mystery, the viewer will expect a crime, a detective seeking a culprit, and a solution. If the movie is a romance, the viewer will expect to see a man and a woman who at first may not like each other but are placed in compromising situations that lead them to fall in love. Mysteries and romances are movie genres. If the writers violate the expected form of the genre, they will probably disappoint their viewers. For instance, if in a mystery movie the detective can never solve the crime because he has overwhelming emotional problems, or if in a romance movie, the man meets a charming woman, falls in love but then she kills him, the genres of the movies will have changed. Similarly, if a jewelry store appears elegant, subdued, rich in materials and style, with concealed merchandise pricing, is somewhat aloof with regard to customer accessibility, and has authoritarian appearing salespeople, the customers will conclude that the jewelry is of good quality and expensive. But if that same store displays cheap costume jewelry with prices boldly marked, has loud music blaring at the entrance, and has unknowledgeable salespeople, the customers' expectations will be much lower. The art of retail store design is therefore most successful when the image of the store coincides with the price, quality, value, level of service, and uniqueness of its product and is consistent with its merchandising, packaging, advertising, management, and sales personnel (Figures 1-1A & B).

The store itself sends a message to its customers. When they see the store for the first time, they automatically and subconsciously register an impression of the store's level of service and quality, as well as the approximate price of the merchandise. The visual cues from which the shoppers make these judgments include the quality of the store's materials, the lighting, the extent of storefront closure, the display fixtures, the signs, the pricing techniques, and, of course, the items for sale. Lesser-quality materials indicate lower-priced merchandise, as does unshielded, glare producing lighting. A well-concealed combination of directional and diffused lighting, on the other hand, emphasizes the quality of the merchandise rather than low prices. Even though a store may sell commonplace, reasonably priced items, it may convey an impression of fine merchandising through its quality lighting and design, and reveal the competitive price of its merchandise only through the prominent display of price tags. To successfully create a congruent image in the mind of the shopper it must tell its story clearly otherwise confusion and lost sales will arise. A closed storefront with small,

A   B

FIGURE 1-1

A store's image should accurately reflect the price, value, level of service and uniqueness of the products for sale. At first impression both of these stores clearly and accurately present their images.

distinctive show windows displaying a few uncommon, expensive items indicates high-priced goods inside. A totally open storefront presents a casual, less-threatening image and suggests moderate pricing. Inside the store, display techniques offer further visual cues. If the products in the display fixtures appear accessible only with the assistance of a salesperson, the merchandise will seem exclusive and expensive. But if products are displayed on flat, open tables, they will appear common and unprotected. Display windows filled with sale signs tell one story while a small, gold-leaf store identification sign on the glass tells another. In short, the way in which merchandise is displayed tells the shoppers more about the store than the merchandise alone could reveal. Unless the shoppers are familiar with the particular items for sale, they will have to evaluate the merchandise closely, check the price tags, and seek help from the sales staff. The other visual cues, such as store transparency, signs, and lighting, send messages before the shoppers even enter the store. It is important, therefore, that external design cues be presented accurately. The overall image of the store must attract shoppers who

FIGURE 1-2
The tone of this gelato store is playful, fun-filled and relaxed.

will be inclined to purchase the kinds of products for sale and also induce them to enter.

Tone is another part of the store's image, and it may be playful or serious, active or passive, exciting or subdued (Figure 1-2). A children's toy store, for example, should be playful or mind-expanding in tone, as should an adult "toy stores," such as an electronics, fitness and specialty gadget stores. A rare-book store, on the other hand, should have a serious image. A store that is visually stimulating or confusing, with multiple levels, detailed written product information, and with all products easily accessible best serves a younger clientele. Older customers might expect easy circulation, no change in levels, more service, and a simple, comprehensive presentation of merchandise. If the store design is visually stimulating, it will attract extroverted shoppers; if the store design is subdued and restrained, it will interest introverted shoppers. Of course, these are generalizations, but a store design is like the home page of a website. Some users are attracted to the clean, restrained, uncluttered elegant appearance of *Time.com*. Whereas others prefer the more sensational look and information of a site like *DrudgeReport.com*. Each is designed to reach a certain segment of the buying population.

A store is a sales tool, like media advertising, telemarketing, or an in-person sales pitch. To be most effective, the store must induce shoppers to enter and buy. The psychology of selling is a subject well known to promotional and advertising people and should be of interest to the store designer, as knowledge of this area, applied to store design, can increase sales.

A good salesperson avoids intimacy with customers. Tom Hopkins suggests that a salesperson should make customers entering a store aware of his or her

FIGURE 1-3
Creating a psychological "toehold" just inside the entrance can facilitate customer movement into the store.

presence and maintain friendly but limited initial contact (Hopkins 1982, p. 174). If the salesperson pushes or crowds the customer, the customer will be more likely to flee the store than buy. The customer should want to ask for the salesperson's assistance. Similarly, a store design must not psychologically crowd or intimidate a potential customer. Indeed, people may have a primal fear of venturing into unknown territory, which shoppers may unconsciously recall when they approach an unfamiliar store. Therefore, it is essential that the store be designed to permit shoppers to determine easy entry and "escape" routes. They should be able to sense the layout of the entire store, if small, or a significant portion of it, if the store is large. This will make the customers feel secure and may entice them to enter. Open, accessible store design can be achieved by providing transparency — that is, a good view of the inside of the store through the storefront — by maintaining lower display fixtures in the front of the store, so as not to hide the interior of the store, and by placing salespeople in positions other than behind a counter at the entrance, facing the shopper. This philosophy of design does not automatically preclude using a completely closed front (having backed showcases and door which must be pulled or pushed to open), but if this is used, one must recognize that walk-in traffic may be limited and a sales tool other than the storefront, such as advertising or word of mouth, may be required to induce shoppers to enter.

The designer must create a store that encourages shoppers, once inside the store, to lower their psychological defenses and become interested in the merchandise. If the customers are relaxed and interested, they may then ask a salesperson for assistance or take the time to evaluate the product themselves and subsequently make the purchase. A small or moderate-sized store should have an interesting display of merchandise located immediately adjacent to the store side of the entrance. This merchandise may not be something that the shoppers will buy, but the display area should offer them a secure place to browse while they develop an understanding of the remainder of the store. It provides a psychological "toehold" (Figure 1-3). When shoppers feel comfortable, they will move on to other areas of the store. Larger stores should be designed similarly but may be broken up into departments. When designing larger stores, it is important to create a sense of free access between the various departments. Wide and highly visible aisles encourage shoppers to move easily to their areas of interest (Figure 1-4).

The architectural elements that determine image have been studied and refined by the most successful merchants, but the rules of imaging are constantly evolving. For example, a simple choice of flooring will create an entirely different shopping experience. Some big box merchants have chosen carpeting for their flooring throughout versus a more traditional hard surface such as vinyl. The

FIGURE 1-4

In larger stores, wide aisles allow some customers to move
freely within the store while others are selecting merchandise.

difference in acoustical properties will be striking to shoppers as will their subconscious awareness of the creation of a more private, restrained environment by the use of this material. While either may be appropriate to a particular store, the choice must be a deliberate and knowledgeable decision by the retailer and the designer.

In addition, images change (Settle and Alreck, 1989, p. 114). When designer labels became popular in the 1980s, they were sold only in higher-quality department stores. Thus the owners of such labeled goods had an image of distinctiveness. Eventually, however, these same labels were sold in discount stores, and very quickly the image of the labeled goods fell from exclusive to common. Similar image changes often occur in materials and lighting design. In the past fifty years, glass block and neon have moved from respectable to "tacky", "kitsch" lighting fixtures and playful geometric shapes have had their impact, and pure monochromatic simplicity has found a home with some retailers. All such trends may fall out of favor for a time, and then be rediscovered, represented and returned to respectability. Designers, therefore, must be aware of the current and future image status of various elements of design. One year's "hot color" or style may be dated and trite the next. Retail store design is as susceptible to trends as are the products displayed in those stores. Many factors affect the complex process of shopping and the development of a retail store image for shoppers. In his book *Influence: How and Why People Agree on Things*, Robert Cialdini cites several factors that subconsciously influence people to take action: commitment, social proof, authority, reciprocation, liking, and scarcity (Cialdini 1984, p. 13). He theorizes that people use such factors as shortcuts in decision making. Three of them — *commitment, social proof, and authority* — can affect store image, design, and operation.

FIGURE 1-5
Entering through imposing, heavy doors like these may add to the creation of a significant psychological commitment in the mind of the shopper.

Commitment is people's desire to maintain consistency with previous deeds or choices. Once they have made a decision, they tend to move ahead automatically, convinced that they have made the right choice. Store designers should also consider this factor of commitment. If shoppers must make an effort to enter the store, this commitment to spend at least some time inside may persuade them to make a purchase. Therefore, the greater the effort required is, the greater the commitment will be. Entering a totally open storefront requires little commitment. Shoppers can step inside, look around, and leave easily. Passing through a closed front with swinging doors, however, requires the maximum commitment on the shoppers' part (Figure 1-5). Of course, any commitment gained by creating a closed storefront may be lost in the smaller number of impulse shoppers who are discouraged by the barrier. The designer thus must decide on the level of commitment appropriate to that store. The transition area (from outside to inside), which sets the tone of the entrance and the resulting degree of commitment, can be subtler than a swinging door. The designer may use an open, arched passageway or a dropped soffit with a storefront recess, or some other architectural device to define the "in and out" boundary of a store. Even subtle transition elements such will help establish a commitment to the store in the shopper's mind.

Commitment may also be created inside the store. If customers can gain

FIGURE 1-6
The sight of these shoppers may provide "social proof" for other shoppers and help persuade to make purchases here.

11

access to a product only with a salesperson's assistance, their level of commitment will be greater than if the item is on open display where it can easily be picked up and evaluated. Also, if customers must ask a salesperson for information about the product, their level of commitment to both the product and the salesperson will be higher, and the chances may be greater that they will buy the product.

Social proof is a factor of influence rooted in the maxim "if everybody's doing it, it must be okay." Aside from word-of-mouth advertising, a store can convey a message of social proof by attracting people into or in front of the store. When seeing many people in a store and not knowing whether they are buying products or only looking, shoppers are led to believe that the store is attractive (literally) (Figure 1-6). Thus, to draw customers, the designer should create areas of interest in the store, such as sale merchandise or special displays, and situate them so that they can be seen from the street or mall. Indeed, establishing social proof may require the designer to create spaces that appear to be filled with people even if they are not. Locating display tables at the front of the store, cramping the circulation somewhat, and packing more displays than would be dictated by normal functional considerations can create a busy area, filled with shoppers. If the products in this area are on-sale, the display may also draw a crowd creating "social proof". If properly designed and merchandised, storefront window displays attract window shoppers, which influence other shoppers to enter. Interesting, colorful, even bizarre displays and lighting techniques attract people to the storefront.

Authority is another factor that influences people's decisions. People do many things simply because they are directed by an authority figure to do so, and store merchants often rely on this principle to sell their products. High-end items, such as jewelry, artwork, and rare collectibles, are often sold to relatively unknowledgeable customers by the "expert salesperson" method. If the store relies on such sales techniques, the store design should convey an image of authority. Such symbols of authority are the use of luxurious, quality materials; showcases in which products are accessible only through the authority figure; and traditional product evaluation areas, which provide face-to-face contact between the customer and the expert, enhancing the store's apparent authority (Figure 1-7). Similarly, the display of wall certificates and other credentials and the establishment of a special office and possibly a raised chair for the chief expert instill the authority concept in the mind of the shopper.

Another relatively unexplored area of image creation is the use of fragrances to influence shoppers. Alan R. Hirsch, director of the Smell and Taste Research Foundation in Chicago, is a pioneer in the science of olfactory research, and he has found that of all the senses, the sense of smell has the greatest impact on human

FIGURE 1-7

*The use of high-quality materials, locked showcases, face-to-face
positioning, and the "expert's chair of authority" will help create the image
of "authority" and influence the customer to believe in the authenticity
and quality of the store and the advice of its "authority" representatives.*

emotions, or "unconscious consumer motives" as they may be called (Settle and
Alreck 1986, p. 33). Because emotions are a strong motivating factor in most
purchases, the relationship of odors to store design is important.

The brain's limbic system is its most primitive part and is the source of
human emotions. Unlike other senses, such as hearing or vision, smells are not
subject to translation and interpretation before reaching a person's limbic system.
Rather, olfactory sensations are received directly by the olfactory nerves and their

connecting fibers in the limbic system. Therefore, people who smell something may be emotionally affected, even though they may not even be aware of the smell. This makes the use of odors to create emotional effects a potentially powerful tool.

There are two ways of influencing shoppers with fragrances, conspicuous and subliminal. Conspicuous odors have been used for many years as a form of olfactoral merchandising. The intent is to use a recognizable smell to evoke a pleasant emotional sensation or memory in the customers (Figure 1-8). Many of

FIGURE 1-8
Customers may recall pleasant memories from childhood through the introduction of inconspicuous aromas into the store such as the scent of flowers in a garden. These smells may make customers more relaxed and comfortable as they shop.

these recalled memories are of childhood experiences, such as the smell of coffee brewing in the morning, bread or pies baking in the oven, or flowers in the garden. Many years ago, one supermarket chain took advantage of this olfactory evoked memory by sprinkling ground coffee on the floors every morning before the store opened. The entering customers could — but only with a conscious effort — smell the coffee. Similarly, real estate salespeople recommend placing a pie in the oven while showing a house, in order to make the house seem more like a lived-in home. Hirsch identified the following geographic differences among regions in the United States in terms of preferred childhood smell associations: East Coast, flowers; South, fresh air; Midwest, farm animals; and West Coast, barbecue. The smell of baby powder is a universally pleasant childhood smell. Conspicuous smells cause people to relax, and so their use in stores can evoke a particular image or mood. For example, a store selling swimwear may introduce the smell of coconut oil; a candy store may use cotton candy; and a lingerie shop may employ a potpourri fragrance. These smells will reinforce the store's image.

Subliminal smells are used in very small quantities and so are virtually undetectable by the customer, although women prefer flowery smells and men favor spicy smells. Such fragrances need not be related to the items for sale. These smells may be used merely to relax the customers and induce them to stay in the store longer, thereby increasing the possibility of purchase. The customers are not aware of the reason that they linger — the odor is only subliminally sensed. The introduction of subliminal smells to affect customer purchasing is becoming commonplace, with different smells introduced by scent delivery machines to accommodate the daily, weekly, or seasonal schedules of different customers.

Finally, to create a particular store image, the designer must consider the type of purchase and the customers' reasons for buying it. Some researchers have suggested that all purchases are emotional and that the role of the salesperson is to help the customer justify an emotional decision. Nevertheless,
the designer must introduce the proper atmosphere for this justification. Some stores may sell products that are obviously impulse oriented, such as small toys, flowers, and candy. These stores should express a playful attitude. Other stores, like those selling consumer electronic gadgets, may retain some of this playfulness and excitement in their image but temper it with "expert" salespeople who can explain the benefits of the product, or offer extensive written explanations of the features of each product. This approach can make an otherwise impulsive purchase seem reasoned. Jewelry, automobile, rare book, fine china, art, and similar stores that sell expensive merchandise should have "authority figure" salespeople in separate rooms, and a relatively quiet atmosphere for the serious contemplation of the purchase. Of course, one person's serious purchase may be another person's

FIGURE 1-9
Symbols and lines create images that convey emotions. Storefronts should match the intended "feel" of the store.

impulse purchase. Therefore, the image rules may be different for the sale of fine jewelry at a luxury resort versus the same sale in a typical regional mall.

Betty Edwards, in her book *Drawing on the Artist Within*, explains that drawings without obvious visible meaning may have a sub-conscious meaning hidden within them (Edwards 1986, p. 112). As such, the lines and surfaces of a storefront may provide an emotional story to the potential customer at that subconscious level. She posits that certain lines and/or shapes convey emotions of power, joy, sadness, calm and other emotions. Designers should be aware of the potential impact these hidden sub-conscious cues. Typical line and shapes with their resultant emotional qualities may be compared to store designs incorporating similar graphic configurations (Figure 1-9) and the reader can judge whether that particular emotion is evident and might influence a shopper. If so, this becomes another factor to consider in the creation of store image.

In summary, store designers must be familiar with all the factors that establish a store's image. Retail stores are successful until the cash register stops ringing, and so the role of the designer is to increase the chances of success by satisfying all the fundamentals of good store design, by creating a correctly imaged store that is functional, services the needs of the owner, enhances the product, and captures the interest of the market.

CHAPTER 2 --- SPATIAL ORGANIZATION

The retail store has three major design elements: display, service, and circulation areas. The relationship or spatial organization of these areas is determined by the same factors that control the layout of any architectural space — the efficient and purposeful accommodation of the space requirements of equipment, products, and people. Unlike most spaces, however, the design of retail

FIGURE 2-1
Corner stores such as this jewelry store are well suited to merchants, who can display many products in the expansive storefront.

stores offers a great deal of freedom from principles or traditions. Whereas other architectural designs, such as those for medical and residential buildings, have many building-code stipulations (light and air requirements, room size, and ceiling heights), retail stores are comparatively less regulated. The main areas of regulation that have the most impact on the overall design concern egress, accessibility for disabled people, energy usage, and more recently, environmental issues. Regulations may stipulate that exit doors swing in the direction of travel, which two points of exit (distant from each other) be provided, that aisles be of a certain width, and so on. Accessibility requirements dictate circulation, product display, and sales transaction fixtures. Energy codes will limit the number and type of light sources to be used. Lastly, concern for environmentally favorable materials may be a code concern or simply a social/marketing preference. Adding to the flexibility of retail design, tradition does not typically dictate design. Unlike offices or institutions, retail store design is less limited by past conventions. Indeed, retailers, landlords, and customers often welcome wild flights of design fancy alike. Construction budgets for retail stores may also permit more elaborate designs than do budgets for residential projects, and so the designers of retail stores often are able to create environments that are both functional and exciting.

The basic space presented to the designer is commonly a rectangle, with the short sides forming the front and rear of the store. Landlords, in both street and shopping mall locations, lease frontage in addition to the total area and, usually try to maintain a balance between the length of the storefront and the total store area. The depth of a front-to-back store is usually not more than three times the overall store depth. Thus, a store with a depth of 75 feet will often have a storefront width of about 25 feet. Corner stores automatically have greater frontages in relation to total area, but this may often as much a curse as a blessing, as storefronts are expensive to construct. Consequently, part of corner-store frontage is often designed as a blank wall. Stores selling products that do not require much space, such as jewelry stores, are well suited to corner locations; others that can successfully merchandise much of their product in large storefront displays, such as shoe or optical stores also are candidates for a corner location (Figure 2-1). Because rents are always higher for corner spaces, the tenant must consider whether the store will really benefit from the added exposure. If not, an in-line location (a store placed between two other stores in a mall) is more appropriate.

The relationship of the areas allocated to display, service, and circulation forms the core of the design of a retail store (Figure 2-2). Unlike other building types, retail stores do not usually separate functional areas by means of walls, except to enclose service and storage areas. Rather, most stores remain as open as possible, to permit the shoppers to orient themselves from any location, and to see

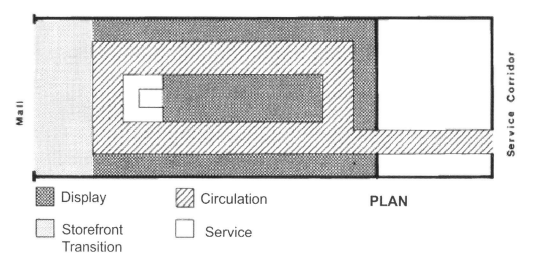

Mall

Service Corridor

▨ Display   ▨ Circulation   **PLAN**

▨ Storefront Transition   ▨ Service

FIGURE 2-2

The functional areas of a typical store.

as many items as possible. Circulation paths in small stores are usually defined by front-to-back or loop aisles, whereas those in large stores may be more extensive versions of basic grids or loops. Circulation paths should be simple and logical. Because the assembled merchandise usually offers a wide variety of visual experiences, creating a complicated circulation route to provide visual stimulation is unnecessary. Such routes should, however, be entertaining and provide a logical sequence for buying. Also, merchandise is typically displayed in orderly, efficient patterns that dictate simple circulation geometry. Overall, circulation must be clear enough that the shoppers will focus on the displays, not on the aisles. If overly concerned about finding their way through the store without bumping into something, the customers will not be able to concentrate on the merchandise and so will not find anything to buy. Typically, the maximum depth from an aisle to a wall that forms a department is no more than 30 feet. If the depth is greater, it may discourage shoppers from entering. Aisles that bend enough to lead the shopper through a series of product experiences controlled by the merchandiser are more successful. These techniques always must be balanced with the shoppers' need to feel comfortable in the space and not to feel trapped in a maze.

The display of merchandise is like a motion picture that requires the viewer, rather than the film, to move. As they pass through the store, the shoppers should feel as comfortable as movie patrons sitting in a theater; their focus of attention should be on the product only. If different floor levels are to be used, the designer must be careful to control the access between the levels with minor stairs or ramps. These vertical transitions should be easy to recognize. It is unwise to design a continuous single- or double-riser stair across the width of the store, as shoppers often move through a store concentrating on the merchandise, and so they may fall or trip over a change in elevation. Also, if the customers are relaxed and not required to think about their movements, the designer influence their actions. But if the customers must climb stairs, the shopping experience will end and the different, more commonplace experience of vertical transport from one floor to another will begin. Any stair that interrupts the shopping experience effectively separates the different levels of a multistory retail shop into different shopping experiences. Each floor is seen as a new "shop." Furthermore, a significant attraction is needed to persuade customers to walk up or down a flight of stairs. Usually these other floors feature destinations—such as discounted items, service areas, or commodity items—where the shopper's goal is targeted. But in any case, it is difficult to continue the first-floor shopping experience to other floors via stairs. The only way that this can be done is by using ramps or escalators that reduce the interruption of the customers' shopping experience. Stairs, even those with only a small number of risers, and elevators distinctly break the shopping experience.

Circulation paths are also the means of emergency egress and so must be the proper width to satisfy building-code requirements. People with physical or visual limitations should also be taken into account. Sufficient aisle space and additional ramps, rather than steps, enable these shoppers to become buyers. People with poor vision appreciate stores with glare-free lighting and aisles that are clearly defined by means of special colors or textures.

Service areas can be either work or storage spaces. Examples are cash counters, wrapping counters, offices, storage areas, tailor and repair shops, shipping and receiving areas, washrooms, and kitchens. Service areas are usually designed for maximum efficiency, accessibility, and optimal equipment placement, and they are generally located at the back of the store, as areas close to the front are too valuable as selling space. In many stores, delivery access also is at the rear of the store. Moreover, storeowners do not want customers entering private areas, and so it is best to segregate service areas to the rear of the store.

The location of the cash counter varies depending on the size of the store, the number of employees, and whether the store is self-service. If the cash counter is at the front of the store, security controls can be increased. But, if the salesperson and cash counter are the first thing that customers see when they enter a store, they may become intimidated. If the cash counter is located at the front, it can be concealed by storefront displays and be oriented to face the store interior. This arrangement, however, requires a relatively wide storefront and presents security problems when only one salesperson is on duty: If the salesperson is serving a customer at the rear of the store, the front cash counter will be unprotected and subject to theft. If the store owner decides to put the cash counter in the front, at least two clerks should staff the store, with one person stationed at the front at all times.

Placing the cash counter at the rear of the store eliminates the problem of immediate shopper/salesperson eye contact and puts the cash counter in a more secure location. This is the best arrangement for single-salesperson stores. The designer must be careful, however, to provide this salesperson with an unobstructed view of the entire store, facing the interior or security may be compromised. The designer should place high display shelving at the store perimeter and may choose to install security mirrors or cameras. Finally, the cash counter may be located in the middle of the store. If the store is large and has many employees, the cashier will probably not need to monitor the store for shoplifters or to control access to stockrooms. The centralized location of the cash counter also provides good access for shoppers. If it can be accommodated, a wrapping counter that is part of, adjacent to, or behind the cash counter is desirable. With the wrapping counter close by, the salesperson need not leave the cash counter unattended to wrap merchandise, which also increases security and speeds sales transactions. Sometimes merchandise is displayed on the cash counter to promote impulse sales, but this requires creative design to avoid negative results. Displays can physically get in the way of cash transactions; and browsers examining the displays can crowd out customers who wish to pay for their merchandise. It thus is usually better to place impulse merchandise near, but not on, the cash counter.

The offices for small stores are generally located in a back storage room and are limited to a short counter, space for a file cabinet, and some shelves. Larger stores may have space for full-size offices, which are also usually adjacent to storage areas or located on a mezzanine. Kitchens for retail store employees are usually Spartan, consisting of small counters with space for a coffee machine, a small refrigerator, and possibly a bar sink and a small table and chairs. Although the number and size of washrooms depend on local building codes, at least one washroom should be provided as a source of water and to eliminate the need for employees to leave the store. In general, unless required by code, and in consideration of security and maintenance issues, public washrooms are not provided in retail stores. Building codes require that if washrooms are provided, then they must meet accessibility requirements for mobility-limited employees. These large washrooms are difficult to accommodate in very small stores. It is more practical that properly designed public washroom be provided in common areas accessible to all.

Display areas are the heart of a retail store. Display is the mechanism that presents the merchandise to the shopper in its most favorable light and that permits the shopper to evaluate and select products for purchase. A display has two elements, product presentation and product evaluation, and the designer must address both. The product-evaluation area is a space directly in front of the display or adjacent to it where a customer may examine the products, read any pertinent information related to it, or have a salesperson explain its virtues. Sometimes the evaluation is a two-step process, as in the purchase of clothing. First the shoppers are attracted to a feature display of a product, and then they select a particular item of apparel displayed on a rack. Next, while standing in front of the display rack, the shoppers remove the item for a closer examination of the product's construction, color, material, and detailing. They may select several similar items as possible purchases and then move to the final stage of product evaluation, which requires them to try on the clothes. In front of a triple mirror, the customers appraise their appearance wearing the product, checking for fit and overall image. After trying on a few other items, they make a final selection and go to the cash counter (Figure 2-3)

Some customers may regard a salesperson in a close side-by-side relationship as uncomfortably friendly. For that customer's cooperation, the salesperson should approach from the front. Other customers may feel uncomfortable when

FIGURE 2-3

After viewing the product on display, the customer removes it from the rack for closer examination, checking color, material, and detailing. Then she will try on the garment and check it for fit and image. If everything is acceptable, she will move to the cash counter.

approached from the front. A retailer/designer discussion of these concerns will help determine the best placement of the salesperson, the customer and the product for typical transactions.

Robert Cialdini (1984, p. 25) describes the influence principle of contrast and its effect on the location of merchandise in a store. If customers are presented with two items, one after the other, their perception of the second item will be influenced by their memory of the first. For instance, after leaving a darkened room, if a person enters a room with average lighting intensity, the second room will appear brighter than if it had been entered under different conditions. Ellen Langer (1989, p. 39) observed that an object appears to be lighter in weight if the holder of the object is first asked to lift a very heavy anchor. Accordingly, sales people should show customers more expensive products first, to make other less expensive, but not inexpensive, products seem more affordable. To apply the principle to the display of similar products, the most expensive items should be located in prominent positions in the store and the least expensive ones elsewhere. Expensive items would be located in feature displays and at eye-level displays. The shoppers will see the more expensive items first and either purchase them or subsequently see and be pleased with the lower price of the less prominently displayed products. Of course, less expensive does not necessarily mean less profit. If a customer can first be sold an expensive item, such as a men's suit, he may also buy lower-priced accessories because he has already adjusted psychologically to the higher price of the first item. This is the main reason that lower-price, impulse items are displayed near cash counters. Impulse items sell easily because they appear inexpensive in relation to the overall expenditure the customer will make. Ideally, merchandise should be arranged in a waterfall of decreasing prices. The customer should be able to view accessory products, displayed in order of decreasing price, as he moves from his main, most expensive purchase to the cash counter. Christina Binkley's *Wall Street Journal* article about navigating a store (Binkley 2010, p. D1) describes a California clothing store that places attractively priced gifts at the store entrance to lure customers deeper into the store toward the more expensive fashions and jewelry at the back. This is a method of attracting unfocused customers particularly for holiday season purchases. Day-to-day customers will most likely have a product for purchase in mind and once in the store will seek out that product.

The retail store usually stocks three categories of products: staples, convenience items, and impulse items, which differ in each store. For example, in a men's store, suits and shirts are staples, whereas ties, belts, and sweaters are often impulse items. Convenience products frequently are common, low-profit items that can be found in most stores; in a men's store, these might be underwear or socks.

Most often, staple items are the items desired by a destination shopper—a person who enters a store with a specific product in mind. Staples therefore should be placed in the more remote sections of the store so that shoppers must pass all the merchandise to get to the point of their destination. Convenience items may be the intended purchase or may be bought as an accessory to the staple item, and so they should be located adjacent to the staple items. Impulse products are not usually a destination purchase but are bought mainly because the customer has entered the store and been impressed with the displays, product, or price of the impulse item. Impulse items thus should be located at the storefront and adjacent to the cash counter (Figure 2-4).

Products that are grouped together are regarded as "belonging" together (Settle and Alreck 1989, p. 83). Therefore, inexpensive items placed in the midst of expensive products take on a more valued perception in the shopper's eyes, and expensive products among inexpensive products lose some of their perceived value. Although the latter makes little sense, the former may be a useful tool. If a $300 watch is displayed in the midst of a series of $2,000 watches, it may be perceived as a "real buy." More commonly, however, the designer/retailer must take care not to mix differently valued items, so as to avoid any problems of customer perception.

As they pass through the store, the shoppers' experiences should be varied in terms of product types, display techniques, and intensity of lighting. The visual experience is sequential, like a movie, and like a good movie, the store should offer action sequences, thought-provoking sequences, and emotional scenes tied together in a logical sequence. Thus, a storefront may be intensely illuminated with colorful displays; the center of the store may be more businesslike, with displays explaining the quality features of a product or pointing out many different types of product; and farther along, displays may be museum-like in quality, evoking a feeling of awe and wonder from the shopper.

Another factor in the design of a store is flexibility of display, which can be divided into two categories—flexibility of store fixtures and flexibility of fixture layout. Because the retail business is constantly changing, flexibility of design is important. Styles and product lines go in and out of fashion in rapid-fire sequence. In addition, regular shoppers and store staff may become bored with a store that does not alter its displays relatively often to create a new look. To allow the store to adapt to new products and styles and make significant display changes, some flexibility must be inherent in the fixture layout. For example, large storefront show windows can be designed to use only movable, temporary display fixtures. Internal display fixtures can be placed on hard-surface floors of wood or tile — heavy fixtures placed on carpeting will leave an imprint. Or fixtures can be

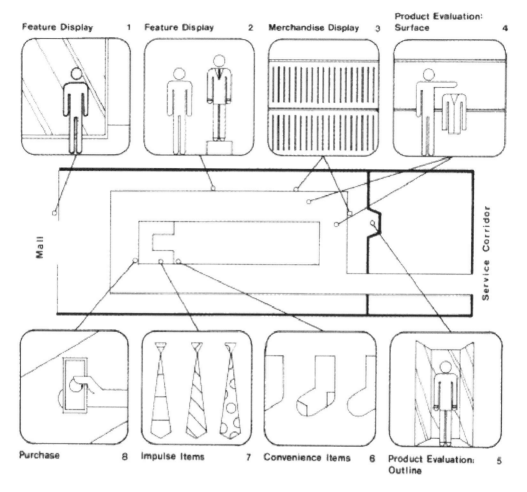

FIGURE 2-4

The ideal customer will follow this sequence of events in an ideal store.

designed to use interchangeable parts, so that they can be used for different products and display techniques. Above all, lighting and electrical systems must permit flexibility. Total flexibility may not be necessary or desirable in all stores, but it certainly should be considered.

In summary, the designer should create a store that has an interesting and flexible variety of details, images, and tones, yet maintains a cohesive expression of the products sold, their price and quality, and the level of service offered. The store layout must direct shoppers along circulation paths that are easy to comprehend and that maximize the exposure of the product in the proper sequence.

CHAPTER 3 --- DISPLAY

Product display is a key element of the well-designed retail store, and it is also the area of design that demands the most involvement by the storeowner. The store designer must listen carefully to the owner's program requirements and translate them into effective methods of product display. If the product is displayed well, it will virtually sell itself, and it will also convey to the customers the store's image, scope of goods, concept, price range, and intent. Individual products on display are like individual letters of the alphabet. Alone, they mean little, but when organized into a pattern and made easily identifiable, they tell a story. Just as a person scanning a newspaper headline immediately understands the top story of the day, so a customer scanning a store with a well-designed product display immediately senses the store's essence and meaning (Figure 3-1).

FIGURE 3-1
The customer viewing this store can easily sense its image from the way the products are displayed.

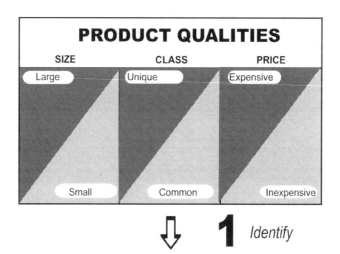

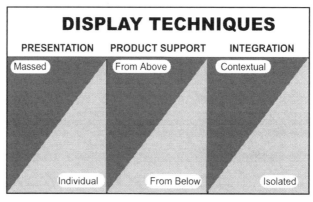

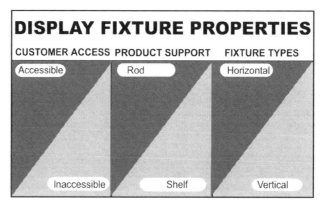

FIGURE 3-2

The final display of a product depends on the product's qualities, the display techniques, and the properties of the display fixture.

Establishing the correct tone for product displays is important, as it acts as an automatic screening that directs potential customers into the store and turns away shoppers with no such interest. The store designer's role is to create well-organized display areas that maximize the available selling space, which, given the annually increasing cost of leasing, retailers do not have the luxury of wasting. The designer's ingenuity in creating and organizing displays can be a decisive factor in the store's profitability.

Display fixtures, like other elements of the store, must emphasize the item, and not detract from it. The customers should be able to understand the product with a minimum of sales assistance. Offering information about the product at the point of display is an excellent idea. The better the customers can understand the product, the greater the chances will be that they will buy it. For this reason, it is desirable to have much of the merchandise accessible to the shoppers as possible. A customer who can see, touch, hear, taste, or smell a product will become more involved and committed to it. Car buyers listen for the special sound of a well-insulated car door as it closes. Prospective clothes purchasers "feel the material"; briefcase buyers love the smell of new leather. Therefore, displays must be designed from the customers' point of view, as the first step in the purchasing process is capturing their interest. This is the primary objective of displays. Display fixtures also have the cross-purpose of defeating shoplifters. Although electronic devices are successful in reducing theft, the proper design and location of certain store fixtures, such as jewelry cases, remain important to preventing crime.

Store display fixtures should also be designed with flexibility in mind, to permit new products or sales methods to be introduced and the store's look to be changed periodically. Remember that many customers who pass by or through a store do so regularly. Without new displays and other changes to attract them, they will become bored with the store and shop elsewhere. In regard to freestanding floor displays, this flexibility may be achieved by using fixtures with interchangeable parts, which can be added to, subtracted from, or manipulated into different shapes. Many manufactured display systems are available that offer this flexibility. Wall display systems accept many different support elements, which can form shelves, hang rods, or hooks. In addition, attachments for metal grid ceilings can be placed throughout a store to create a changeable ceiling display system. The process of developing effective product displays consists of identifying the product's qualities, selecting the best display techniques, and incorporating them into the final display (Figure 3-2).

PRODUCT QUALITIES

Each product has inherent qualities—size, class, and price—that to a great extent dictate the way in which it will be displayed. The extremes for these qualities are large and small for size, unique and common for class, and expensive and inexpensive for price (Figure 3-3).

Size. Large products such as furniture, rugs, and pianos are easy to see and

PRODUCT QUALITIES		EXAMPLES
Large ● Unique ● Expensive		 Antique furnitures, cars
Large ● Unique ● Inexpensive		 Christmas trees, ceramic tile
Large ● Common ● Expensive		 Automobiles, televisions
Large ● Common ● Inexpensive		 Garbage cans, rain barrels, golf bags, luggage
Small ● Unique ● Expensive		 Fine rings, watches, rare coins and stamps, perfumes
Small ● Unique ● Inexpensive		 Hand-crafted items, craft jewelry
Small ● Common ● Expensive		 Cell phones, hand-held electronics
Small ● Common ● Inexpensive		 Calculators, pens, candy, office items

Photos credit this figure: Hemera

FIGURE 3-3
Examples of categories of product qualities

may be displayed some distance away from the customer. They do not necessarily have to be placed in a storefront show window. Large products do, however, require a generous amount of space if they are to be displayed properly (the same amount of space the customer would deem appropriate if the product were placed in the home), as well as enough circulation space around the display to permit the shopper to view it from all angles (Figure 3-3). Large products may be grouped or displayed individually, but they must always be considered in terms of the revenue they generate versus the area they occupy. Because large, low-profit products occupy more space and return less income, using only a sample of large, inexpensive merchandise, is more sensible than displaying a complete array. Delivered products (items that the customers actually buy, as opposed to floor samples) are then stored elsewhere. Large products should form the backdrop for smaller products, as large items still can be seen around the perimeter of the display. Moreover, extremely large products, such as furniture, appliances, home-improvement tools, and pianos, are difficult to relocate, which may result in stagnant, permanent displays if flexible displays of smaller products are not placed nearby.

Small products, such as jewelry, eyeglasses, and coins, are hard to see and so must be brought close to the shoppers' eye level to attract their attention. Products like jewelry are best displayed close to the front of the store in cases at eye level. Small products may be displayed individually but need more intense lighting than do large objects, since there is less surface to reflect light. If greater visual impact is desired, small items can be grouped together to form a large, eye-catching mass. If small products are not massed in display, however, they will present a maintenance problem — small items are easy to steal. In addition, if the shoppers are permitted to handle the display merchandise, they may return the product to the display without concern for its position or relation to other objects, making it necessary for store personnel to be constantly rearranging the products on display. For these reasons, small, individually displayed products should be available for evaluation only with a salesperson's assistance.

Because they are so easy to relocate, however, small products allow for flexible merchandising. They return more income per square foot of leased space than large objects do and so should be placed on display rather than stockpiled in a storage area. Of course, the number of products to be displayed and the type of display fixtures to be used depend on the size and other features of the product.

Class. From a display standpoint, unique products are those that are one of a kind, are of limited quantity, are unusual, or have attributes generally unknown to the public. Such products include jewelry, rare coins, artwork, custom-made goods, unbranded items, unusual items such as gadgets or special tools, and living products such as pets and distinctive plants or flowers, and sometimes even fruits or vegetables. It is difficult for cost-conscious shoppers to evaluate the price of such special products because unique items often have subtle qualities that set them apart from similar products. Their prices thus may be based on these special qualities as well as their inherent value. The price markup on rare or unusual goods can be considerable because the real value is not easy to determine; it may be based on such intangible qualities as rarity, beauty, quality, construction, or faddishness. The "sizzle" of products like jewelry or artwork sells more often than the "steak." Buyers are buying the uniqueness of the product.

To sell the "sizzle," unique products usually require more explanation of their attributes, either in written form or from a salesperson. Greater effort is required to display rare and beautiful objects. Special lighting or individual display cases may be needed to highlight the qualities of the merchandise. Unique items may be impulse or destination products, but generally the shoppers are familiar with the store but are probably not aware of the specific items for sale until they review them at the store. This is different from the purchase of such common items as newspapers, name-brand clothing, or appliances, which are true destination products.

Common products are those that may or may not have special attributes, but in any case their attributes are so well known that only little display effort or verbal or written information is needed to sell them. The differences among similar items produced by several manufacturers are small; sometimes the only way to distinguish one common item from another is by its advertising or promotional program, such as generic aspirin versus Bayer. From a store designer's viewpoint, however, both kinds of aspirin are in the common class.

Common products may also include items that would be unique but for the extensive shopper awareness of them. Electronic equipment, home appliances, and other such items often have special qualities that distinguish them from similar products. But because the attributes of such products are well reported by consumer product reviewers, advertised in the media or online, or made known by word of mouth, their distinctive qualities are assimilated, and the products become common commodities. An example of this transition occurs when an exciting new electronic device is placed on sale, often with great fanfare. When it is first introduced, it is unique, but its qualities rapidly become known to the shopping public. Eventually the product becomes so well known that it can be sold simply on the basis of price. No special display or explanation was required to sell it— what was first unique became a common item.

Common items may be displayed in groups of similar or different items, or they may not be displayed at all. In the latter case, only a sign may be needed to notify shoppers that the products are available. Displays of common products are intended, first, to indicate availability and, second, to state the sale price. Even considering these simple requirements, however, displays of common products need not be boring. Though the individual products are commonplace, they may be displayed massed or in sequence to provide visual excitement.

Price. Products range in price from *expensive to inexpensive*, and each extreme requires a different display treatment. Items that are both expensive and unique must be carefully displayed to make them also look expensive and unique. Likewise, products that are both inexpensive and common must reflect these qualities when on display. People should be able to judge the relative prices of a product from the way in which it is displayed (Figure 3-4). If customers are shopping for price only, they may lose interest in a display that looks expensive, even if they do not see the price. Similarly, shoppers looking for unique items may be misinformed by a display that seems to cheapen the product. Price is a relative factor, based on one product's price compared with those of similar products.

Price also affects the prominence of a product display. More expensive items probably have a higher markup and should therefore be sold in more extensive and elaborate displays. Less expensive and bargain items can sell themselves in

FIGURE 3-4
Customers should be able to judge the relative price of a product by the way that it is displayed.

simple displays. Robert Cialdini observed that ironically, higher-priced products may induce shoppers to buy more than they would if the same items were discounted (Cialdini 1984, p. 15). He believes that whenever possible, people make decisions based on routine patterns of action and that most people may have a patterned, automatic response that dictates the purchase of more expensive items on the assumption that they provide a higher level of quality. In other words, shoppers may buy a product more rapidly if it is overpriced than if it is discounted. This theory may be valid only with regard to unique products, however. People may be more inclined to buy common products based on the best price because they are aware of all the product's features or because they know that there is no difference among brands. On the other hand, customers may buy the most expensive wine—a unique product—solely because of its high price. Consumer knowledge of the product is the key to proper product pricing. Manufacturers of brand-name, heavily advertised, common products have been very successful at persuading shoppers to buy their higher-priced items instead of the cheaper generic items. In effect, these manufacturers attempt to establish a unique quality in an otherwise common product by creating a brand. A product may, for instance, become the "Mercedes of paper clips" to justify the difference in price between it and similar, less expensive paper clips. In this case, the high-priced paper clips, although not in the unique display class, could be displayed prominently to distinguish them from the lower-priced ones.

According to Settle and Alreck (1989, p. 83), items that are placed close to one another become "grouped" in the consumer's mind. Therefore, an inexpensive item amidst expensive goods gains a perceived additional value, and an expensive product amidst low-priced goods loses some of its value. Care should be taken not to confuse the consumer. Displays should present a coherent statement regarding price. One could say, "Don't mix the Rolex with the Timex." Designers should also know that products placed near eye level have a higher perceived value than do those placed at waist level or below.

DISPLAY TECHNIQUES

Presentation. After the designer evaluates a product to determine its size, class, and price, the proper display techniques of presentation, product support, and integration with related products must be determined.

Products may be displayed either in a mass or alone, based on the most significant quality of the product: its class. If the product is unique, it should usually be displayed to enhance its individuality. A fine painting, for example, should be distinctively shown on a wall, with no other paintings above or below it.

Similarly, individual attention should be apparent in the display of fine fur, jewelry, pottery, or rare coins.

Common products often benefit from mass presentation, arranged by product color or type or a combination of the two. For example, a shop selling fresh vegetables may group them by color rather than size. This kind of display creates a strong mass of single colors, which is attractive and also helps the shopper find a specific item. Massing products by type offers more visual impact than could be generated by isolating the individual item. Mass displays can be effective in

A

B

FIGURE 3-5
Products may be displayed in mass to create visual impact.

clothing stores to create a significant display impact for products that are difficult to display such as men's ties. (Figures 3-5 A & B).

Products that are neither unique nor common can be shown in mass groups with a single product featured at the front. A mass of colorful teapots, for instance, may have one teapot specially illuminated and positioned in front to detail its features to the shopper for evaluation. In this type of display, the individually displayed item functions as a display sample while the mass of products behind is the stock. A massed display of products may be effective even if the products are only generically similar, such as televisions. A spectacular mass-display effect can be achieved by setting all the different sizes, makes, colors, and styles of television sets to the same channel, with a result similar to that of a large kinetic sculpture. Expensive items are sometimes presented in mass displays, but most often inexpensive or moderately priced products are shown in this way. Expensive items are usually isolated in individual displays to enhance the product's uniqueness and justify the higher price to the shopper. Large items, too, are less often massed than are small items, which often need the visual impact of massing.

Product Support. Product displays can be further defined by their method of physical support. Merchandise may be suspended from above or supported from below with, for example, a hook or a shelf, a hanger or a pedestal, on the ceiling or the floor. The designer's choice of support depends on the object's physical qualities and the kind of emphasis desired. Large or heavy items, such as furniture or pianos, can be supported from below by the floor. Other items that cannot easily be hung from above, such as bottles, books, and bowling balls, belong on shelves. Handbags should also be presented on shelves rather than hooks. Tennis rackets, paintings, and dresses all are shown to best advantage when supported from above. Tennis rackets do not stack well and are better hung from hooks; paintings are cheapened by a shelf display, and dresses collapse into a wrinkled lump unless they are hung from above.

Some items may be displayed either way, depending on their packaging. Thus men's belts may be displayed hanging or, if packaged, may be stacked on shelves .A designer shop may hang all its items of apparel, to accentuate their qualities. A discount clothing store, however, may pile its items of apparel loosely on a table to emphasize that the garments are common and inexpensive.

Integration. Inexpensive items frequently are priced higher because of their special packaging. Such small, common items as buttons, screws, or electronic parts— which would be grouped in a bin if loose —can be hung from hooks if they are specially packaged. The products should be displayed with the largest face out,

FIGURE 3-6
Contextual displays help the shopper select combinations of products.

to give the shoppers easy access. Special packaging and hanging displays often can magnify the product's price many times. The packaging and handy display make the customers' selection easier, and their concern for price will be overshadowed by this convenience. The trend away from shelf displays in favor of hanging displays of common items has been a significant retailing event over the years and is the result of better packaging methods. Today, almost all impulse items are packaged and hung on display, which is a better display method than the former practice of grouping small products in a visually indistinguishable mass on a shelf or bin.

Those products that can be displayed in either way should be shown, as they would be typically seen by shoppers outside the store. Thus, shoes are displayed supported from below, and hanging light fixtures, wall clocks, purses, and men's ties are typically viewed supported from above

The final display technique is product integration. Products may be shown singly or grouped with related products. For example, a men's tie may be displayed with other ties but without regard to other related items of men's apparel, or it may be displayed on a mannequin with a contextual display of tie, shirt, suit, belt, and hat. Similarly, a vase may be presented alone or with flowers in it; dinner plates and cups may be isolated or be accompanied by utensils, place-mats, a tablecloth, and table.

The choice of isolated or contextual displays may be based on the impact of a contextual display. If the product would sell well from an isolated, non-integrated display, then it should be displayed in that fashion. Contextual displays consume more space and are more expensive. Of course, a common bar of soap need not be displayed in a soap dish, and a pair of men's socks can usually be shown alone. But if the soap is in the form of a carved duck or if the socks are knee high and patterned, then both products might benefit from a contextual display. Contextual displays help the customers make a purchase. Most people are inadequately trained in visualization and need some contextual integration to help them select products offered in a variety of styles or colors. Men's clothing is a typical area for contextual displays (Figure 3-6). Because men's wear is often purchased by women for men and women cannot try on the product, contextual displays are important sales tools. This same logic applies to women's lingerie departments, where men do some of the purchasing. If customers see a contextual display, such as a room attractively wallpapered for display, they may buy the product. If, on the other hand, they see an isolated roll of wallpaper, they may not be able to make a decision and so not purchase the item. The sales power of contextual displays is immense, as customers want to have their decisions made easier. Featured items, such as new or sale items or high-profit items, are frequently shown contextually.

Jewelry, vases, hats, eyeglass frames, and other products that the customer can easily visualize or try on may not require a contextual display. But some products, like cosmetics or perfume, are so personal that they may be "displayed" only on the individual customer.

DISPLAY FIXTURE PROPERTIES

Display fixtures must be designed or selected to accommodate the product's qualities and so may be chosen after the appropriate display techniques have been determined. Each display fixture has three basic properties: It allows or excludes customer access; it permits the product to be displayed from a rod or a shelf; and it is horizontal or vertical (Figure 3-2).

Access. Display fixtures either give shoppers access to the product or permit them to view the product but restrict their ability to reach it on their own. Whether self-service or customer assisted, stores usually have both accessible and inaccessible display fixtures. Several factors influence the designer's selection of display fixtures: product security, danger, fragility, and uniqueness. Security requirements are based on the price of the product in relation to its size. That is, small and expensive objects are in demand and easy for shoplifters to conceal. Large products are more difficult to steal, and cheap products are not worth the risk to steal. Not surprisingly, jewelry, coins, cameras, watches, electronic storage devices, cell phones and other small electronic gizmos are generally placed in fixtures that are not accessible to shoppers.

Another reason to limit access to a product is if it is hazardous. If the product could injure someone who grabbed it, its display fixture should prevent access. Guns, knives, saws, and animals should be kept under lock and key. Products that may be damaged by improper handling should be accessible only under a salesperson's supervision. Fragile artwork, crafted glass and pottery, rare coins or books, and even fragile flowers such as orchids fall into this category. Or a storeowner may decide that certain unique products should be inaccessibly displayed. A display that requires the customer to ask permission to see a product makes the item more exclusive and, therefore perhaps, more desirable. Any rare or distinctive product may qualify for this attention. Whole areas or rooms can be made accessible only to escorted customers, such as fur vaults, wine cellars, and special display salons. Restricting customer access is used as often as a sales technique as it is for security purposes.

Support. As discussed earlier, products can be supported from above or below, with rods or shelves. The rod may also be a hook, arm, pin, or clip, and the shelf may also be a bin, box, rack, platform, or pedestal. Once the support has been chosen, the best technical solution must be determined in consideration of the other display factors.

Fixture Types. Display fixtures can be either horizontal, like an island or counter display, or vertical, placed up against a wall or forming a wall. Horizontal displays, such as those shown in Figure 3-7 are frequently used for feature displays

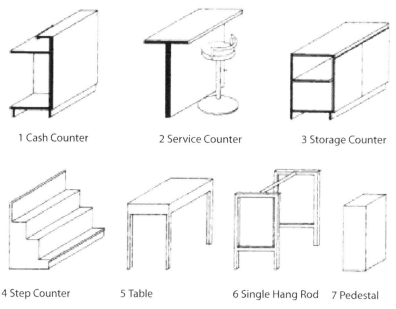

1 Cash Counter   2 Service Counter   3 Storage Counter

4 Step Counter   5 Table   6 Single Hang Rod   7 Pedestal

FIGURE 3-7
Typical horizontal display fixtures

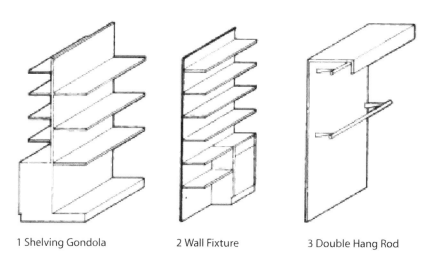

1 Shelving Gondola   2 Wall Fixture   3 Double Hang Rod

FIGURE 3-8
Typical vertical display fixtures

and impulse items. Because they are low in height and do not obstruct the shoppers' view across the store, horizontal fixtures can be placed in the center of the store in the highest traffic areas— that is, the best areas for feature and impulse item displays. Horizontal fixtures can be used as sales or wrapping counters and are ideal for the sale of products that require a salesperson's assistance. The salesperson can explain or demonstrate the product from across the top of the fixture while the customer stands or sits in front. If both large and small products are sold, the larger items should be displayed in taller fixtures at the perimeter walls, thereby permitting shoppers to see the entire store.

Vertical fixture displays, such as those shown in Figure 3-8 are excellent for products that need a background, such as paintings or products with sculptural qualities. They may also be successfully integrated with continuous overhead soffit lighting. Products such as books, shoes, and boxed items can be successfully displayed vertically. Vertical displays also permit a concentrated stacking of modular and non-modular products displayed from knee height to a point overhead.

Horizontal Fixtures. Cash counters are the salesperson's island of refuge, the "business end" of the display floor, where a sale is consummated, and often the point of sale for accessories or impulse purchases. Typically, the space allocated for cash counters is small because space must be devoted to sales first and therefore the counter must function very efficiently. The size of the counter is determined by the equipment, wrapping spaces, and storage it must accommodate, the size of the products to be handled, and the maximum number of store personnel who will work behind the counter at one time. In additional special counter space and approach requirements to meet Accessibility codes must be considered. Cash-counter equipment includes wrapping equipment (knives, scissors, tape dispensers, staplers, and so on); telephones and intercoms; cash registers; calculators; security monitors, if necessary; and charge-plate devices. Storage must be provided for blank and completed credit-card receipts, bags, boxes, wrapping paper, and office supplies. The counter space for wrapping merchandise must be adequate; often, a back counter is used so that wrapping does not slow sales transactions.

Service display counters are used to present products that require a lengthy demonstration or explanation, such as jewelry or cosmetics. The customer is seated in a chair or stool and the countertop functions as a desk. The countertop and front are usually glass and the products inside are not accessible without the help of a salesperson. Light fixtures are often installed in the case to solve an otherwise difficult lighting problem.

Storage display counters are similar to service display counters but are used for briefer sales demonstrations, and so no seating is provided for the customer. Instead, the area below the display is used for storage.

Step counters resemble a short flight of stairs and consist of a series of adjacent display platforms, rising one above the other. They are used to display taller products with a backdrop and provide greater separation and isolation of products than do the flat surfaces of service or storage display counters. Step counters may be glazed to control access or left open.

Tables are un-serviced, fully accessible horizontal displays. They are typically used as center islands and often contain feature or impulse items. The height of the tabletop depends on the height of the merchandise sold; essentially, the customers should not have to bend down to reach the product being sold. Small items such as paperback books are displayed on a table 30 to 36 inches high, whereas larger items, such as bicycles, are displayed on a lower table, such as a platform 8 to 12 inches high.

A single hang rod is a low-height horizontal rod suspended at either end by a self-supporting post or panel. Casual clothing such as sportswear is usually hung on this type of unit. The rod can be mounted at different heights to accommodate items of varying sizes. For example, men's suits are typically hung on a 42-inch rod, slacks on a 54-inch rod, and overcoats on a 63-inch rod. A 54-inch rod is selected most often because it is low enough to see over but can display several different items of apparel at once. Sometimes the fixture has a series of stepped-down hooks that form a waterfall island display.

Pedestal displays are featured elements used to isolate and highlight specific products. A pedestal may be a full-height mannequin or a flat surface supporting a product or a partial mannequin. Pedestals can be constructed at different heights and grouped together to form multiple-feature displays.

Vertical Fixtures. Shelving gondolas are vertical shelves used as island

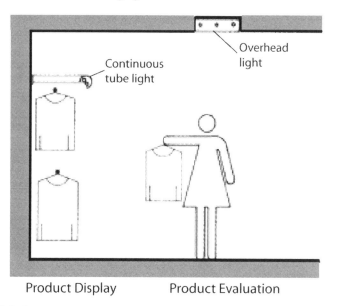

Product Display   Product Evaluation

FIGURE 3-9
The lighting of double-hang rod fixtures must provide even illumination for product display and for the adjacent product evaluation area.

displays and are tall enough to display merchandise clearly without obstructing a view of the entire store. They do not form a wall but are commonly used back to back. In place of the lower shelves, gondolas may have a storage unit for empty boxes or stock merchandise; the unit may also have its own light sources.

Wall fixtures are full-height vertical units that commonly contain either shelves or hooks for display or lower storage areas instead of shelves or hooks. Typically, wall fixtures have continuous overhead soffit lights.

Double-hang-rod fixtures are the workhorse displays of clothing stores. They are located on perimeter walls, or if used as back-to-back islands, they effectively become perimeter walls. Triple-height racks are sometimes used in price-oriented stores; if so, a catwalk must be provided for access to the top rack. The lighting of double-hang-rod fixtures and the position of the rod must be well designed. The lower rod should be 3 inches forward of the upper rod, and a continuous soffit lighting fixture should be placed about 6 inches in front of the edge of the lower product to illuminate both racks evenly. Adequate illumination must also be provided in front of the racks to facilitate product evaluation (Figure 3-9).

Display Fixture Materials. Display fixtures may be constructed of almost any material. Glass, wood, and plastic or metal laminate are commonly used because they are relatively easy to construct into the many different shapes required for display. Almost any other material, however, may be used to construct displays. Marble, granite, cast iron, glass, concrete, metal, brick, and tile all have been used with varying degrees of success. Sometimes a designer may want to achieve a contrast between rough display surfaces and the fine surfaces of the product for sale. Although such contrast often produces an interesting effect, the designer should be aware of the potential problems. In general, the display surface should not compete with or physically damage the product. Fine watches, for example, cannot be displayed on a rough concrete surface without risk of breakage. The design of display fixtures offers great freedom of expression, but the designer must present the product properly in order to attract shoppers. The product and the user must be carefully considered, with elaborate fixture designs often yielding to practical requirements.

The designer may use either stock or custom-designed and -built store fixtures. Stock fixtures are available for almost every type of case a store might require and are usually, but not always, less expensive than custom-built cases. When the budget permits, however, using well-designed custom fixtures can be important to establishing the store's image. Custom fixtures can also provide creative display solutions for small or unusually configured stores. In addition, custom fixtures are easier to integrate with the store's other design elements— the storefront, walls, and ceiling—to create a unified design.

Few solid-wood fixtures are used today because of their prohibitive cost. More commonly, wood veneers are laminated to less expensive core materials, such as particleboard or plywood. Hardwood (oak, walnut, teak, and so forth) and laminated-surface display cases are constructed in a similar manner. Cabinets come in three classifications of quality, as established by the Architectural Woodwork Institute (AWl): premium, custom, and economy grade. Premium and custom-grade cabinets use higher-quality materials and construction than do economy-grade cases. Custom-grade materials are usually specified for store cases. The designer should review the AWl's standards (available in the AWl book Architectural Woodwork; and ensure that the cabinetmakers follow the AWl specifications when constructing the store's cases. The AWl makes the following suggestions to designers regarding cabinet-grade fixtures: Indicate grain direction to achieve the design effect; consider field-joint locations and fastening methods when developing construction drawings (not as an afterthought); clearly specify hardware function requirements; use a scribe (a reducible section) at the ends of cabinet work that abut walls to accommodate the inevitable "out-of-square" room; avoid "feather edges" or acute angles at cabinet outside corners; provide cutout dimensions and locations for electrical, electronic, and plumbing facilities; and recognize installation problems, such as door and elevator clearances for delivery to the site, wood-blocking locations in walls for cabinet support, and items and finishes that must be installed in the shop instead of the field.

Wood-finished display fixtures are warm, rich, and durable. They cost about the same as plastic-laminate finishes, and so the decision to use one or the other becomes one of aesthetics and durability. Hardwoods are traditional and may be used successfully to display almost any product that requires a conservative look. If the wood grain competes with the fine detail of some products or a more contemporary look is desired, woods or plastic laminates may be used to finish the fixtures.

Softwoods such as pine and fir are used with solid-material construction to create fixtures with a more casual appearance. Softwoods can be painted, stained, or finished with clear varnishes. However, softwoods dent easily, are not very durable, and do not permit precise detailing. In addition, softwoods are not dimensionally stable; they grow and shrink under different temperature and humidity conditions.

Plastic and metal laminates are popular finishes for display cases. In addition to providing a durable, hard, and easy-to-maintain surface, they are available in many different colors and textures. Laminates may be bent to form curved shapes and are dimensionally precise and stable, two characteristics necessary for high-quality cabinetry. Corners on laminates can chip and this factor should be taken into consideration by locating cabinets to avoid impact or by providing corner guards.

Glass used in the top or sides of the fixtures displays products while limiting access. Glass can also be used for cabinet doors, shelves, or the structural material of the cases.

Display Fixture Construction.   Display cabinets with doors can be finished with a variety of detailing techniques. Opaque or transparent materials can be used for swinging or sliding doors and many different types of hardware are available as well.

Swinging-door hinges may be either exposed or concealed. Butt, wraparound or pivot hinges, the traditional types of exposed hinges, are easy to install, strong and moderately priced, but they are, of course, visible when in place. "Invisible," or concealed, hinges must be mortised into the cabinet and door and thus are difficult to install; European-style concealed hinges, which can be surface mounted, are easier to install but are more expensive than and not as strong as "invisible" hinges. Nonetheless, European-style hinges are quite popular, because they are concealed, require no catch, and provide a clean, uncluttered look when used with flush overlay cabinet construction. Cabinet pulls are available in a multitude of shapes, sizes, and materials. If a contemporary look desired, simple wire pulls or their plastic counterparts may be used. For a very clean look, pulls may be eliminated by installing concealed finger recesses at the top or bottom of a door.

Sliding-door hardware consists of the tracks in which the doors slide with pulls or rings used to move the doors sideways. Sliding-door tracks may partially or completely concealed by the cabinet material at the top and bottom but will be visible when the door is opened. Door tracks may be made of aluminum or plastic and come in a variety of anodized finished or plastic colors. Sliding-door pulls may be surface mounted or recessed into the door.

Frameless glass doors require hinges and tracks specially designed for that purpose. Glass hinges may be center pivot or offset pivot. In the center-pivot design, a short channel is affixed to the top and bottom of the glass. Attached to the channel is a pin that is set into a sleeve embedded in the cabinet; the hinge pivots in this sleeve. This type of hinge requires no drilling through glass and therefore permits easier adjustment. The offset pivot does require a hole to be drilled in the glass. Small round plates are set into the glass and attached. The side of the cabinet receives the other half of the hinge, and the two are attached, interlocked, and held in place with a pin. For a smoother operation, glass sliding doors glide in aluminum tracks on ball bearings. Because the lock mechanism is fully exposed,

---

45

however, it is difficult to lock the glass doors unless sliding doors with push-button locking are used. For hinged glass doors, conventional cam locks may be installed in the glass, or a solid hinged panel that swings in front of and partially covers the doors may be used to keep the doors closed. This solid hinged panel hides the inner parts of the cam lock normally exposed through the glass doors.

Drawers require glide hardware and pulls. Drawer glides are rated according to load capacity, mounting, and extension. Load capacities range from 50pounds to over 100 pounds per glider, with the standard commercial designation at 75 pounds. Glides may be side, bottom, or top mounted. Side mounting is the standard configuration for drawer glides. Top mounting is used for under-counter drawers, bottom mounting for pull-out shelves. Glides can extend the entire drawer body out of the cabinet (full extension) or extend all but 4 to 6 inches of the body (standard extension). Glides are available that permit drawers to be self-closing, to lift out, and to prevent unintentional opening. Sliding-drawer pulls are similar to door pulls and may also be eliminated for flush designs by using concealed finger pulls.

The construction of cabinets with swinging doors or drawers falls into four different styles: conventional flush with face frame, conventional flush without face frame, flush overlay, and reveal overlay. In conventional flush construction, with or without a face frame, the door and drawer faces are flush with the face of the cabinet, permitting the use of different drawer and door thickness. This style is expensive, however, because of the narrow gap tolerances between doors, drawers, and frame, which require precise woodworking to maintain an even gap. Eliminating the face frame saves some material and labor costs.

Flush overlay construction provides a clean, contemporary image. The cabinet frame is not visible unless the doors or drawers are opened. Drawers and doors are located in the same plane, separated by a small gap that creates an almost continuous surface plane.

Reveal overlay construction is similar to flush overlay but provides a half-inch standard reveal between the edges of drawers and doors.

Many stock components can be used to display merchandise effectively, including a variety of adjustable brackets and standards for product support. Standards for adjustable brackets are either surface mounted or concealed. Both designs are similar and consist of a rear-mounted steel channel with a regular pattern of vertical slots designed to receive and interlock with a bracket. The bracket may be attached and relocated vertically anywhere on the standard. Various attachments, which permit these systems to be used for wood or glass shelves and as hang-rod supports, can be affixed to the end of the bracket. However, because the wall must be furred out so that the standards can be mounted behind the projecting wall, concealed standards are expensive to construct. (Furring is creating a space between the base wall and the projecting wall with wood members or metal furring.) In addition, the walls must be properly blocked before the standards are installed; the standards are designed to accommodate reasonably heavy loads, which the wall also must be able to support. Brackets are available in stock designs that, though functional, may not satisfy the designer's aesthetic requirements. If this is the case, custom brackets can be fabricated by combining chrome or brass tubing with a bracket adapter.

Adjustable shelving and rod displays may also be constructed by using pilaster standards and brackets. These standards mount on the side walls and have small clips that fit into horizontal slots to hold a shelf or a rod. This type of system is typically used inside cabinets or cases with vertical dividers. Other adjustable systems consist of slotted hardboard designed to support a series of different shelf and hook brackets. If the stock wall materials are not acceptable to the designer, this type of system can also be custom built to the desired specifications.

Stationary hooks and brackets are another option for wall mounting. There are several well-designed lines of colorful plastic products from which to choose. Or custom brackets can be designed and fabricated relatively inexpensively with chrome or brass and concealed plate mountings. Standard metal tubes and connections can be used to make three-dimensional display grids supported by the floor, wall, or ceiling. Products can be hung from the grid or placed on shelves. This system offers the benefit of flexibility, as the displays may be taken down, redesigned, and reconstructed easily to give an area of the store a new look.

The success of any fixture design depends on the correct interpretation of the store owner's intent, knowledge, and direction. The storeowner therefore should know the best display techniques for the merchandise and suggest these to the designer. The designer must incorporate the owner's direction and the size, weight, and color of the product into the fixture. Store fixtures are precisely designed selling machines. In consideration of the store's ever-increasing operating costs, store fixtures must display the product with a minimum of wasted space. Smaller stores, more than large ones, require the designer to be creative in developing display fixtures. In a successful display, every inch is used efficiently.

CHAPTER 4 --- STOREFRONTS

The front of a retail store serves several functions. First, it acts as a symbol of the store—its merchandise and philosophy. Second, the front attracts shoppers to the store. It provides a filter or lens through which the designer can control the shoppers' perception of the store. Last, it provides a physical transition from the street or mall to the store's interior.

From a distance, the storefront is the one physical connection between the shopper and the merchant. Therefore, the store's concept and merchandise must be clearly reflected in the design of the storefront; otherwise potential customers may pass by, not understanding the store. Unless the shoppers are prompted by advertising or a previous shopping experience and already have the store in mind as a destination, their interest must be captured. Even if shoppers are willing to try the store because of advertising or other recommendations, they may, upon seeing the storefront for the first time, decide not to enter if the front does not fulfill their expectations. For example, if shoppers expect to find a discounted jewelry store but the storefront image makes the store appear expensive, they may become intimidated or disappointed and leave.

The storefront must give shoppers an unmistakable impression of the store's price range, product, service, selection, degree of sales assistance, and level of quality and the type of shopper the store is attempting to attract. Properly selected materials, signs, views of the interior, product displays, and control of access through the entrance will facilitate the customer's understanding of the store. The difference between a store with a limited window display of products without visible price tags surrounded by finished stonework, as shown in Figure 4-1 A & B, and a store with an open storefront displaying massive amounts of merchandise is evident. With one look at each storefront, shoppers have a complete grasp of the product, price, and type of service each store offers. They can judge whether this store can satisfy their needs and the needs of those like them.

The storefront captures the shoppers' attention and invites them in to look at and perhaps buy the products or services for sale. If the front is properly designed, one quick look will tell shoppers if the store's philosophy is what they are seeking. But this is not enough. The front must draw all potential buyers. Well-designed stores are also attractions. Through a combination of form, materials, lighting, signs, and product display, the designer can create a magnet pulling the proper customers to the storefront.

The designer and the display manager have complete control over what passersby can see inside the store. The storefront acts both as a filter to screen out store elements the designer does not wish the shoppers to see, such as services areas, and as a lens to focus attention on the elements the designer does wish the shoppers to see — the products for sale. In the storefront, opaque and transparent surfaces combine with controlled lighting and well-designed product displays to enhance both the product and the store's image.

Finally, the storefront is a transition area between the street or mall and the store itself. This transition space must meet the shopper's expectations. If a customer expects exclusivity, the transition area must be designed to control the

A

FIGURE 4-1
Shoppers can sense the operation, pricing, and the intended market segment for a store simply by looking at the storefront's materials, signs, and overall design.

B

flow of people into the store. If the shopper expects the store to attract the general public, the transition into the store must be easy and open.

STOREFRONT DESIGN

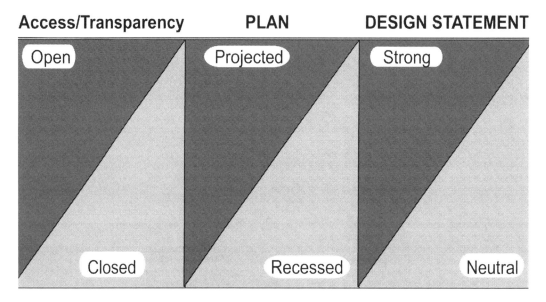

FIGURE 4-2
The three main components of storefront design.

STOREFRONT DESIGN

There are three main components of storefront design: transparency, the plan, and the design statement (Figure 4—2).

Access/Transparency. A storefront elevation design can range from a completely open space, both physically and visually, to one that is completely closed. Open storefronts have no physical elements separating the street or mall from the store proper (Figure 4-3). In effect, there is no front except for a sign band or sign above the storefront opening. This type of storefront can be achieved in an enclosed mall as well as a street environment. Creating a completely open front in an enclosed mall environment is simple because weather concerns are not a problem. But even in a street location, open fronts are possible. A canopy or awning can shield the store from precipitation, and if necessary the interior temperature can be maintained through the use of an air curtain at the storefront. (An air curtain is a continuous source of forced air that flows down at the line of the storefront, thereby creating an invisible barrier to heat transmission.)

Open storefronts reached the peak of their prominence in the enclosed mall shopping center. In the late 1960s and early 1970s, the use of open storefronts for stores in malls was widespread. Since that time, however, their popularity has moderated and many shopping malls do not permit them at all, for three reasons. First, most malls are now designed as a street concept, as opposed to a department-store concept. In a street concept, the stores are assembled in a mall as a well-defined group of independent merchants connected only by a neutral, street-like, enclosed mall passage. The designers of these malls attempt to replicate the feeling of an outdoor shopping street within an interior space. Therefore, the use of open storefronts on such a "street" may destroy the image the developer is trying to create. Conversely, many of the earlier enclosed malls were designed in the department-store concept, in which open storefronts were both acceptable and encouraged by landlords. These shopping centers had a mall that was more of a department-store aisle than a street. Within this aisle, kiosks (island stores) were

© VikaValter

FIGURE 4-3
Totally open fronts encourage browsing and invite passersby to enter but lack a definable image.

© Giorgio Fochesato

FIGURE 4-4
The completely closed front presents an image of exclusivity and conceals much of the store interior. Destination oriented.

permitted, creating—in combination with the open storefronts along either side of the mall—an image of one large department store. The second reason that open storefronts have declined in popularity is that most totally exposed stores are not as handsome as they could be with some strategically located screening. Storefronts filter out the less attractive areas that inevitably exist in a store, such as sales or storage areas and the backs of counters and other display fixtures. The third reason for the decline of open storefronts is the security problems they pose. An open design makes it very difficult to monitor exits and gives shoplifters a wide, uncontrolled escape route.

The other extreme is the completely closed storefront (Figure 4-4). In theory, this storefront has no visual or physical openings from the mall into the store. The front is a barrier between the mall and the store. Show windows are backed; doors are kept closed and are constructed of opaque materials. This type of shop is oriented to the destination shopper and provides an exclusive image. Few completely closed fronts are constructed, however, because of the importance of informing the shoppers outside the store of the experience they will have once inside the store. Most storefronts are designed to be a mixture of open and closed, with only a few at the extremes.

Open storefronts offer the greatest ease of entry for browsers and the least opportunity to state the store image or to filter out or feature various store elements. Closed storefronts make it more difficult for casual shoppers to enter but offer the greatest possibility for image development and for screening out or magnifying store elements.

Shoppers usually see the storefront and store interior as they walk along the mall or street only a few feet from the front. Thus, passersby have an oblique view of the store that may last only a few seconds, and so the storefront must catch the shoppers' attention at their first glance. If the front permits a view deep into the store, the shoppers' angle of vision will be increased, extending their viewing time as they walk by. This factor should be considered when the elevation is designed. There are several ways to provide an extended view into the store: open-backed showcases, storefront recesses, and glassed-in or open entrances instead of opaque doors. Eliminating the front showcases is another way of widening the viewing angle.

Plan. The plan of a storefront in relation to the building face or fascia—the horizontal band above storefront doors and windows, on which a sign is often placed— may show the storefront as either projected or recessed. Most storefronts in malls are aligned flush with the fascia above. However street shops often have projecting elements, such as bays or awnings. For many years, projecting storefronts (with the tenant's lease line extending beyond the fascia or building wall above) or other projecting architectural or sign elements were not permitted in enclosed shopping malls. Now developers of enclosed malls seeking a variety of storefront experiences, typically permit a variety of projections.

In shopping centers that do not permit projections, most merchants will build their storefronts to the lease line in order to use every bit of their expensive leased space. Consequently in these centers, the main differences among storefront designs will be limited to differences in materials and in the amount of storefront transparency. Storefronts become two-dimensional. To combat his limitation, projected storefronts and three-dimensional storefront elements provide a greater variety of storefront designs. To achieve a projected storefront, the tenants' leasable area includes a 3-to 4-foot rectangle of space in front of their store, into which elements of their storefront may project. There are many different methods of projecting the storefront, the most common of which are display bays, awnings and canopies.

Recessed storefronts are common in traditional in-line street locations and less-often in enclosed malls. Such areas in on traditional retail street are designed to display merchandise away from the glare of the sun, to permit shoppers to look into the store from an area protected from the weather, and ultimately to draw customers into the store. In almost all cases, however, these reasons for recessing are not valid for retail stores in an enclosed mall. That is, the lighting is usually controlled by the mall architecture to shield the storefront from direct sunlight, and the problem of weather is eliminated by the enclosed location. The only remaining traditional reason to use a recessed front is to draw shoppers into the store, by easing the physical transition from mall to store. Major storefront recesses usually contain significant product displays; the intention is for the shoppers to be sold on the front product, to follow the line of product into the storefront recess, and then to be drawn into the store proper. Minor storefront recesses may be used to give a three-dimensional quality to storefronts even if projecting stores are not permitted or possible. With minor recesses, bays can be formed; entrances can be emphasized; the entire front can be recessed, and a canopy can be placed overall, extending to the building or lease line.

Design Statement.   The design statement or look of a storefront is the identifiable pattern formed by all the design elements together. These patterns might be labeled traditional, contemporary, bold, cutting-edge, theatrical, minimalist or gimmicky. The design statement depends on a myriad of factors, including the overall store concept, the product for sale, and the location of the store.

—

First, the storefront design should reflect the entire store. Store designs are best when they are consistent, integrating details, materials, and colors inside the store with the storefront. The shoppers should be able to anticipate the design of the store interior after seeing its exterior. In addition, the design statement should be one that will be fashionable throughout the term of the store lease. Retail store designs are subject to rapid changes in trends and fashion, and both the public and the retail industry take a dim view of an outdated store. Designers have several choices: They may attempt to break new ground by establishing a new look; they may ride the crest of a design wave that they hope will last as long as the lease of the store; they may use a classic traditional design; or they may work with traditional materials in a neutral, low-key manner. To a great degree, the length of

© RiverNorthPhotography

FIGURE 4-5
Restaurants often employ strong storefront design statements and bold signs to tell their retailing story. Except for wafting smells, the essence of tasty food and excellent service cannot be clearly revealed by exposing the interior of the store to potential customers outside.

FIGURE 4-6
A neutral storefront design statement (in this case a fully glazed storefront) permits the interesting and colorful products to become the major visual statement.

time that a design is likely to remain fashionable is related to its intensity. If the design is entirely neutral, it cannot go out of fashion because it has no fashion. But if the design statement is pronounced, the risk that it may fall out of fashion is greatly increased.

Any design concept may become either a strong or a neutral statement. A design can merely suggest, with the right materials and geometric forms, a classical, retro or historical atmosphere or it can attempt to replicate it. A general guideline for making a design statement is to establish a strong design only if the product itself is a weak sensory experience and will not have a significant visual impact from a distance or if the store concept is more important than the actual merchandise is (Figure 4-5). If the product has something to say, however, it should become the most important element of a storefront and the store design statement (Figure 4-6). Most products can provide a great sensory experience if properly displayed, and so the design statement of most storefronts should be more neutral than strong. The strategy is simple: Sell the product, not the storefront. In most cases, this strategy works. But if the product is more service-oriented such as insurance sales, process-directed such as customer-created arts or crafts, or tech-oriented requiring product demonstrations, it may not sell itself, and therefore a strong design statement may be necessary to compensate for this lack of product impact. If the product has strong olfactory but limited visual impact, such as prepared food, the smell of the product should be sold (within the limits of any lease agreement regarding odors), along with a strong design statement. A moderately strong design statement might be appropriate to products that are common and not visually overwhelming and cannot be grouped to form a strong visual statement, such as cosmetics.

STOREFRONT ELEMENTS

Whether the architecture of a storefront can be classified as neutral or strong or somewhere in between, three elements are present in every well-designed storefront: display, transition, and identification.

Display Elements. The display elements of the storefront permit shoppers to see the merchandise for sale under the best possible conditions. Products may be displayed at the storefront in built-in show windows that are part of the storefront construction or in store fixtures placed against a storefront window or opening. Show windows may be constructed with or without backs. If non-backed, the show window will permit the shoppers to see beyond the displayed merchandise into the store; if backed, the show window will focus the customers' attention on the displayed product.

The smaller the product is, the more likely it will have to be displayed very close to the storefront. Most jewelry, for example, must be displayed in the storefront, whereas larger products, such as furniture, may be effectively displayed away from the storefront. The focus of storefront displays should be approximately at eye level to be most effective, but the elevation of a feature storefront display should relate to the height at which the product is typically viewed—that is, hats should be displayed slightly above eye level, shoes substantially below.

The designer must determine which product, if any, will be featured in the storefront. The importance of displaying these products must be weighed against the shoppers' needs—as they stand outside the store—to know what is inside. Shoppers want to know what to expect when entering the store; without this knowledge, they may be unsure and choose not to enter. Thus it may be equally important for the storefront to offer a view into the store, to indicate the store's overall size, layout, selection, and services. To solve this problem, storefront jewelry, for example, may be displayed in non-backed showcases or in viewing windows adjacent to the show windows (Figure 4-7).

Not all stores require storefront display showcases. It may be enough simply to enclose the entire storefront with clear glazing, giving passersby an unhindered view of the store's merchandise and the store's layout. In this approach, products may be displayed in changeable, temporary displays at the storefront glazing without significantly reducing the view into the store. The storefront should provide a suitable frame for the merchandise of the store, either one large frame to enclose the view of the store and all its merchandise or several smaller frames to accentuate feature displays at the storefront. In either case, the frames should have forms, colors, and materials that relate conceptually to the product sold and focus the shoppers' attention on that product. The storefront frame should, in general, not compete with the product. Just as a modern print would not be displayed in a baroque frame, the latest in electronic equipment, with its crisp machined metal and smoothly formed plastic parts, should be framed with visually and psychologically compatible materials, finishes and colors—*think* Apple Store. Both the modern print and the electronic equipment should have a simple, neutral frame. The store frame should also be thoughtfully detailed, for poorly designed or executed details detract from the product displayed. Ideally, the materials and forms of the storefront should relate to the overall design of the store and provide a visual and physical transition into the store.

Storefront lighting for product display is critical. The key rule requires lighting at the storefront to illuminate something important. This object to be illuminated will most likely be the product; it may be a sign; or it might be the storefront itself if a strong design statement is required. But it will not be the floor.

FIGURE 4-7

*The storefront displays small
products at eye level and provides
the shopper a clear view into
the store.*

FIGURE 4-8

*Veiling reflections in the display
window of this store make it
difficult to see the merchandise.
Awnings or recessed glazing
can help eliminate this problem.*

Designers often place high-intensity lighting aimed at the floor of the storefront, which detracts from the show window as well as the product displays, by drawing the shoppers' eyes away from the product. In most cases, the product at the storefront should be brightly lighted, and the lighting system should be flexible. Depending on the requirements of the display, this system may include adjustable and fixed lighting, as well as lighting from above, below, to either side, or from the front or back. Show window designers use many effects to attract shoppers to the window. Exceptionally bright lights draw attention, as do light fixtures with colored filters, which can be used to create unusual product display effects. Storefront display lighting must be able to accommodate changes in the types and styles of product to be shown there. A few rules of lighting should be observed as well. Storefront lighting should not spill out into the mall, and the light sources (direct glare) should not be visible. Light should not fall on the storefront glass. If the light is directed toward the glass, it will become visible and act as a barrier between the shopper and the store. If the store is outdoors or even in some indoor locations, direct sunlight may fall on storefront glazing and create glare and veiling reflections. To eliminate this problem, a canopy or awning should be provided, or the glazing should be recessed from the path of sunlight (Figure 4-8). Storefront display areas can also have flexible systems of hanging displays from the storefront ceiling or soffit and should have electrical availability at each show window or display area in multiple locations to provide flexibility.

The security of storefront displays must also be considered. Shoplifting is one of the shortcomings of a totally open storefront; products that are easy to grab will, unfortunately, be stolen. Protecting merchandise in an open storefront often becomes more expensive than the cost of constructing a closed store. Shoplifters are rewarded by poorly secured storefront merchandise; they can grab merchandise and be on their way without even entering the store. Thieves can also reach around a non-backed, open display case or hook small items such as jewelry through the unsealed joint between lights of frameless glass. The battle between the shoplifter and the storeowner is unceasing, and the designer should give as much consideration as possible to security. Electric devices and methods can be incorporated in the storefront to announce a person entering the store or to indicate the unauthorized removal of products. These devices, coupled with secure displays and strategically located cash counters or desks, can decrease the incidence of shoplifting.

Transitional Elements. Transitional elements in a storefront are the forms and materials such as the doors, gates, grilles, and arches that define the passageway between the street or mall and the store interior. Although these

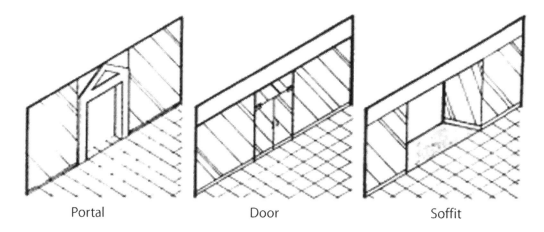

Portal   Door   Soffit

FIGURE 4-9
Typical storefront transitional elements.

elements and their effects may be subtle, they are nevertheless important. Transitions help develop the store's identity, help create a sense of commitment to the store in the shopper's mind, and announce the entrance of the store. Shoppers must be aware that they are entering a store if they are to establish a relationship with the store, to identify and remember it. Imagine an enclosed mall filled entirely with open storefronts. Shoppers could move from store to store with no sense of transition. In these conditions, their recollection of shopping would be a blur even if they had bought something. To establish an identity, storefronts must create a tangible sense of transition. Moreover, identification and recall enable the shoppers to return and to advertise the store through word-of-mouth recommendation. Transition areas also create a sense of commitment in the shoppers' minds. When they enter the store (and a good transition element will give them this feeling of entrance), they subconsciously make a commitment. It may not be a commitment to purchase something, but it may be strong enough to make them look seriously at the merchandise. Even a vague commitment is better than none. Some people even feel compelled to buy something once they have entered a store, although this level of commitment is probably rare.

The transition may be subtle, such as a change of flooring, wall, or ceiling material from mall to store. Or it may be a change in geometric form, such as a drop in the ceiling or the placement of solid entrance elements in an otherwise transparent storefront (Figure 4-9). Traditional entrance forms include arch, post-and-beam, and pediment openings, with derivatives of these forms commonly used to mark the retail store entrances. A swinging door alone can create a definite sense of transition in a shopper's mind. Entrances that are open and require no physical effort from the shoppers to enter need some form of architectural treatment to announce the transition. Although transitional elements are important to a storefront design, the transition should not become a forbidding barrier to the shoppers, recognizing the major point of the storefront is to invite them into the store.

Identification Elements. Identification elements enable shoppers to recognize, remember, or identify a storefront even if they have never been in the store. The most common identification element is the sign giving the store's name and logo. The landlords of most shopping centers, enclosed and strip, restrict the placement of signs. For many years, as a reaction to some tenants' overzealous sign designs, signs were restricted to a single fascia above the store entrance, and the choice of sign technique for use in a mall was usually very limited. But the trend has been toward more freedom in the placement and style of merchant signs. In many enclosed malls, merchants are now restricted only to using quality materials within a certain sign area. Previous restrictions on sign length, letter height, position in the storefront, and letter type are being dropped in favor of encouraging sign design creativity and diversity. There has been the development of sophisticated back lighted box signs and sculptural, minimal, blade, and any other sign variations. For retail stores outside on a street, local sign ordinances may control the sign design. These vary greatly from jurisdiction to jurisdiction but are usually more concerned with size than location or technique.

Because the signs in many malls have been limited to the name of the store, with regulations often prohibiting signs from listing the items for sale, prices, or any other promotional material, signs have become less significant as a device to draw shoppers into the store. For this reason, store signs have frequently become only a graphic symbol to be recognized and remembered. Some retailers have become very sophisticated and confident and have reduced their front signs to minimal proportions. Successful symbols may even be unreadable, but many retailers strive to use the same symbol consistently throughout all their advertising and packaging. The store sign must, therefore, be easy to recognize as the store symbol. Ideally, its letter style and look match the printed symbol that appears on the store's packaging and advertising. In general, the more often the symbol is used, the more important it will become. A tenant with a national chain of stores will be more concerned about sign clarity and consistency of graphic display than the single store owner will, who may be inclined to use a more obscure or minimal sign, as the sign's symbol has limited exposure.

In many cases, the sign takes a back seat to the storefront, the product, and the overall image of the store as an identification element. Apple's white and glass minimal look, Bass Pro's overall design, and White Castle's building are at least as important as their signs in terms of store identification.

Glazing.   Storefront glazing may be used as an entrance, window, or finishing material. Although glazing is usually transparent, it may become noticeable if it is improperly designed or installed. Poorly detailed glass, glass subject to reflections, wavy glass, or dirty glass will impede the shoppers' view of the store. Properly installed and maintained glass, on the other hand, attracts customers with its crispness and sparkle.

Exterior glass panels and the framing methods to be used must be analyzed for wind and impact loading by an architect or structural engineer. Some manufacturers of storefront glass and metal systems have developed wind-load tables for their systems, which the designer can use to create a storefront that will withstand local wind conditions. For indoor locations, glass size may be dictated by transporting concerns: Door and elevator sizes, and other interior elements that might block the passage of glass from the truck to the installation site, must be considered.

Exposed glass edges should be ground and polished, whereas edges that will be framed need not. Polished edges take one of two forms, either a pencil edge (rounded) or an arris edge (chamfered). Glass may be sandblasted or acid etched for different graphic effects. Clear glass may be spray painted any color on the back, to create opaque colored glass. If opaque, geometrically patterned glass is desired, it may be patterned rather than polished.

Safety glass is glass that has been treated or processed so that it either resists breaking or breaks into small granules rather than large, jagged shards. Tempered and laminated glass are both forms of clear safety glass. Safety glass is used in hazardous locations, which include all heavily trafficked areas and any place where there is a high risk of impact. Federal regulations stipulate the required location of safety glass in storefronts. Designers of storefronts may want to consider using safety glass in all public areas as relatively inexpensive, permanent insurance against harm to customers.

Float glass is the glass typically used in most construction. When ordering float glass, the designer must specify either clear or tinted glass. Tinted glass is not recommended for retail storefronts, however, as it reduces the customers' view of the merchandise and affects their color perception. For framed interior glass, 1/4-inch float glass is most often used.

Tempered glass, a safety glass, is a heat-strengthened float glass that is many times more resistant to impact breakage than untreated float glass. Tempered glass may be used in a storefront without mullions that is, framed only at top and bottom. In this type of frameless installation, 1/2-inch glass is generally used, although 3/8-inch glass may be used on smaller panels. It may be necessary to fill joints with clear silicone or use stiffener clips between the panels of unframed tempered glass, to maintain proper alignment between glass panels and to reduce waviness. Unless the installation must be weatherproof, or resist wind loads, or if the potential misalignment of the panels is a concern, the joints frameless glass typically need not be sealed with silicone. Large panels (over 12 feet) of tempered glass are available, but only certain American manufacturers are capable of producing them. Therefore, additional construction time and cost will be incurred unless one of these special manufacturers is located near the project area. Smaller panels of glass can usually be tempered locally.

Tempered glass cannot be reworked after it has been tempered. All edges must be ground; all holes or notches must be cut; and the glass panel must be cut to the exact size of the opening before it enters the oven. This means that tempered glass cannot be ordered until the major framing elements of the storefront are in place and the opening sizes can be measured. Tempered glass is also subject to spontaneous breakage. On rare occasions, glass panels virtually explode and disintegrate without warning. The reason for this spontaneous breakage is not known, but it does not present any substantial hazard to the public unless tempered glass is placed overhead.

There are two methods of treating glass, and in both cases, the glass is placed in a heat-treating oven. In one method, the glass is held in place in the oven, gripped with tongs at the top. But this process leaves tong marks in the finished product and also causes a more uneven glass panel to be produced, as the glass bends, stretches, and curls in the oven. The unevenness caused by this process is generally not a problem in smaller panels of glass, and tong marks are a problem only for glass that will not be framed. If the edges are to be exposed, the designer must specify that the tong marks be located at the top or bottom and buried in the frame; if edges are to be exposed, the designer should specify the float method of tempering, which produces a superior product. With this method, the glass is floated in the oven on a current of air. No tong marks are produced, and the glass is not distorted, as it is heated more evenly as it is strengthened.

Laminated glass consists of two or more panels of float glass with a plastic sheet or sheets bonded between them. Laminated glass is a safety glass that is substantially weaker than tempered glass, but has its own special breakage feature: Upon impact, laminated glass breaks, but the plastic sheet inside it holds the panel together. This makes laminated glass especially suitable for overhead glazed areas. Laminated glass may also be curved in sizes suitable for use in storefronts, although this is an expensive process. Unlike tempered glass, laminated glass may be cut or ground after lamination.

Glass block is a glass material that is laid like masonry. It may be used in a storefront to provide a translucent, decorative, solid barrier. Glass blocks are available in several sizes and in clear or opaque finishes, as well as finishes that are reflective during the day and transparent at night. Glass block is an expensive but interesting glazing material, not suitable for display use. Large areas of glass block may impact floor-loading capacity in multi-storied buildings.

Closures. Sliding doors may be made of opaque materials like wood or metal, as see-through grilles or as glass doors. Sliding doors either hang from an overhead track or rest in a bottom track. Rollers are located in the bottom or top track, and the doors slide to one side or the other along the tracks. Sliding doors may be bi parting—separating in the middle—or slide in one direction only. Panels may slide behind each other or separate into pockets recessed into the storefront. If a large opening is to be accommodated, however, the stacking space and resulting pocket construction required for the panels can become objectionable, as it takes up expensive floor and storefront space.

Sliding-glass storefront sections are generally constructed of tempered glass and aluminum framing sections. Standardized framing systems are available that consist of variously shaped and sized aluminum components. Aluminum finishes can be obtained in anodized black; light, medium, or dark bronze; and clear. Baked-on paint finishes may also be applied at the factory to create almost any color. Frameless sliding storefront sections are also available that consist of top and bottom aluminum rails, containing the rollers or guides that hold in place sections of tempered glass. The top rail of these panels may be concealed in a soffit to enhance the frameless look. Frameless sliding doors are available in sizes up to 12 feet if bottom rollers are used to support the door; top-hung doors are available only in smaller sizes. Locks in frameless sliding doors are placed in the bottom rail, which is an inconvenient position for opening and may be difficult for employees to handle. Frameless sliding-door installations are not weatherproof, however, and so may be used only indoors. In addition, sections of glass gap when the door is closed, inviting thieves to hook merchandise through the opening. Moreover, sliding doors cannot be used as fire exits unless they remain open during store hours; and because they must remain open all day, they are useful only in enclosed malls or other places with regulated temperatures.

Swinging doors may be made of solid or transparent materials or grilles. Swinging doors give the storeowner a choice between keeping the door open or letting the shoppers open it. The swinging feature enhances the sense of transition into the store and cuts off street noise or other objectionable environmental conditions outside the store.

Swinging glass doors may be framed in aluminum sections of narrow or wide profile. Frameless 1/2-inch tempered-glass panels with top and bottom rails or bottom rails and top hinge patterns may also be constructed as doors. When top hinge patches are used, unframed glazed transom panels may be placed over the door to create an all-glass, mullion-less front. Frameless swinging-glass doors may be as high as 12 feet, but doors in constant use should not be higher than 8 feet.

Swinging entrance doors are normally hinged at the top and bottom with pivot hinges rather than leaf hinges. Doors may be offset or center pivoted, depending on the situation. Closers with hold-open features are typically used on swinging doors; in the better installations, such closers are concealed either in the floor or overhead. If the closer is to be concealed overhead in aluminum framing tube, it must be center pivoted. Closers may be set to hold doors open from 90 degrees to 180 degrees. If a 180-degree swing is desired, offset pivots and closers must be used.

Sometimes it is desirable to install a swinging door in the face of a storefront that will not provide public access, such as a door into an office or storeroom. In this situation, a concealed door is required, and it is possible to design a door that is unnoticeable to all but the most observant passersby. In this fashion, the store's service requirements are fulfilled, but not at the expense of the storefront design.

Overhead security closures include overhead rolling doors and grilles. Overhead rolling doors are composed of interlocking aluminum slats that may be rolled into a coil and stored above the ceiling or pulled down on side tracks to create a solid door. Tracks are mounted to solid structural surfaces or to steel tubes that extend from the floor to the structure above. These doors are available in anodized aluminum finishes or factory finished paint. Sometimes the door is constructed of unfinished mill aluminum, but the tracks and bottom rail of the door are anodized to enhance the appearance of the storefront during the day. Overhead grilles also roll on tracks but are made of round horizontal bars joined and separated by vertical links in a grid pattern. Doors are available with clear plastic inserts between bars that provide additional security. When closed, grille doors without plastic fillers do not block air circulation or the overall view of the store, but they do offer security. In addition, grilles are usually less expensive than rolling doors.

Overhead closures do not waste valuable floor area, as they require only a small space for the side tracks and the bottom rail. Overhead rolling doors and grilles are usually installed in stores located in shopping malls, as the doors remain open during the hours of store operation and provide no weather protection. Some jurisdictions require exit doors to be placed in grilles or doors, to permit emergency egress when the overhead door is pulled down. Other regulations require the door to be manually operable from the inside as well as automatically operable, to accommodate the needs of any employees who remain in the store after business hours.

Overhead doors are either manually or electrically operated, although doors more than 10 feet wide should be electrically operated so that they do not overwhelm store employees. Two control panels that operate the motorized door are necessary, one panel outside the store and one panel inside the store. Both panels are usually located near the storefront, with the controls keyed to provide security. Metal enclosures to house the rolled-up grille may be purchased for overhead doors, although this enclosure is usually not necessary. It is often a requirement, however, that grilles be enclosed with a fire-rated gypsum board and metal stud barrier. Access panels must then be provided at appropriate locations to service the enclosed door and its motor.

Side closures include side-coiling or accordion-folding grilles. Side-coiling grilles operate like overhead-coiling grilles, except that the coil is placed at the side of the storefront rather than overhead, and the grille slides along overhead and bottom tracks. Side-coiling grilles are usually motorized and require only a minimum of floor space. Side-folding accordion grilles are similar to side-coiling grilles but fold into a pattern approximately 8 inches wide instead of coiling when opened. They slide along a top track and are pulled or pushed manually. Pockets must be created within the storefront architecture to accommodate the door when it is open. Accordion grilles are less expensive than coiling grilles; both types are available in the same variety of finishes as are overhead grilles.

Finishing. Many different finishing materials may be used in storefront construction to frame the storefront openings, provide a sign background, or create a solid surface. The key quality desired in any material used for this purpose is durability, as the storefront receives intense physical contact from shoppers and cleaning personnel. Appropriate materials that can take abuse are metal, hardwood, glass, tile, brick, and stone. Other possible materials are plaster or integral-color plastic laminate on particleboard. Plastic sheets, exposed gypsum board, or softwood may be used for areas that are not subject to physical contact, such as sign backgrounds. A durable material such as metal, stone, or tile should always be provided for the base of the storefront, as this area is subject to constant kicking and contact with floor-cleaning equipment.

Signs. The store sign is an important element for sales in a typical retail store. Unless the retailer relies solely on the store and merchandise presentation to attract customers, a store sign is necessary to provide identification. Typically retailers establish, through advertising, the store as a destination for shoppers. When shoppers do have this destination as a goal, the retailer should make the search as simple as possible, which implies a readable and easily visible sign. The landlord of a mall or strip center may dictate the type of sign, but some guidelines have general applications.

The sign should fit the image of the store. If the store image is traditional, the sign should be constructed of natural wood or brass. If the storefront is glass and metal, neon or edge-illuminated plastic letters may be appropriate. The sign should also be readable. Ideally, it should duplicate the print-advertising logo, and so this logo should lend itself to that use. Careful consideration should be given to letter style, sign color, size, and background surface color. Contrast between the sign letters and the background must be sufficiently pronounced to permit easy identification. This is especially important for retail stores in street or strip center locations, as shoppers literally locate their destination store while driving in their car. The fascia signs of a strip center thus become the equivalent of a directory in a mall. Finally, the retailer should consider reserving an adequate budget for the sign. All too often the sign is the last item purchased and is therefore subject to the "economizing" that often occurs at the end of a project. This is unwise because the sign—together with the storefront and the product presentation—is a major tool to attract customers into the store. Signs for retail stores are usually custom-designed and fabricated to the letter, style, size, and material requirements of the tenant. There are two types of signs: individual letter signs and panel signs. Both may be

Individual letters: Non-illuminated   Panel sign: Non-illuminated

Individual letters: Silhouette illuminated   Individual letters: Neon illuminated

Individual letters: Illuminated   Panel sign: Illuminated
translucent face

FIGURE 4-10
Typical retail storefront sign types.

either internally or externally illuminated (Figure 4-10).

Individual, non-illuminated letter signs may be constructed of many materials, but the most common are wood, plastic, or metal. The individual letters may be cut from sheet material or, in the case of plastic or metal, formed or cast into shapes. Cut wood letters are usually 1/2 to 1 inch thick, whereas saw-cut plastic and metal letters may range from 1/8 to 3/8 inch thick. Formed or cast letters can be made to any practical thickness. Wood letters may be painted a color or stained and clear finished. Plastic letters have integral color. Metal letters may be painted or made of anodized aluminum, or the base metal may be mounted directly to and flush with the background surface or set away from the wall on pins. Pin mounting is useful if the sign background surface is an irregular material, such as brick or stucco. Sign letters may also be pin mounted on smooth background surfaces to achieve a floating effect.

Non-illuminated individual letters also include painted gold- or silver-leaf letters, other painted letters, and "non-dimensional" or very thin die-cut letters, which are usually applied directly to both sides (front and back) of storefront glass. The size and placement of decal letters is frequently restricted by shopping-center owners. Lettering is typically set adjacent to doors at eye level to provide easy store identification. Small (3- to 4-inch) "non-dimensional" letters are also effective if repeated in a pattern just below eye level. In some cases, this serves the dual purpose of identifying the store and helping shoppers avoid walking into the storefront glazing. Care should be taken to ensure that background surfaces or objects do not detract from the legibility of signs placed on the storefront glazing. Individual non-illuminated letters may be floodlit or silhouetted in front of an illuminated surface, such as storefront glazing, or sandblasted or etched into the storefront glazing.

Individual, illuminated letter signs include those with translucent faces, silhouette type, and exposed neon letters. Translucent-face sign letters are at least 8 inches high and are typically fabricated from sheet metal or cast metal for the letter frame and translucent plastic for the face of the letter. Inside the letter, a cold cathode tube (fluorescent lamp) is bent and fitted to the shape of the letter; the back of the letter is sealed with metal. Alternatively, LED lamps are used in line to provide illumination providing for more compact placements and increased energy efficiency. The translucent plastic face is available in many colors; many shades of white can be obtained from the cold cathode lamp as well. For consistency, light sources in all sign letters should be of the same type, color, and intensity. Translucent-face letters are usually mounted directly to a sign background without pins. Electrical ballasts for the sign, junction boxes, and disconnect must be concealed behind the sign background, and these require access panels for servicing.

Silhouette signs are composed of individual letters that are channel-sectioned, die-cast, or made of sheet metal and then pin mounted about 2 inches away from the background surface. Cold cathode tube lighting is placed in each letter, and the light from this tube bounces off the background, providing a halo effect for each letter. The letters are readable in silhouette under low or night-lighting conditions. The effectiveness of silhouette signs depends on the reflectivity of the background material. The greater the reflection is, the greater the contrast between the sign surface and the background will be. However, too much reflection (such as a mirrored surface) is not desirable, as it may reflect the lamps within the sign instead of the sign itself. The minimum height for silhouette and translucent-face letters is about 8 inches because of the limitations of forming and placing the cold cathode tubes. Fasteners, attachments, and all electrical devices for translucent-face and silhouette signs should be concealed. Manufacturer, underwriter, or union labels should not be exposed to view.

Neon signs are the third type of illuminated, individual letter signs. Neon is a colorless, chemically inert gas that glows reddish orange when placed inside a sealed glass tube and charged with electric current. Neon tubes are of thin diameter and, unlike cold cathode tubes, are not coated inside with phosphor. Other gases, such as argon, helium, krypton, and xenon, may be used in addition to or mixed with neon to produce other colors. The inside of the glass tube can also be coated with a translucent color. Neon signs are playful and creative, as the glass tubing can be bent in many different shapes and can be used for signature and pictorial graphics as well as simple letter forms. Neon signs may be set in front of an opaque or behind a clear glass sign background—either method is effective. However, protection for neon signs must be considered, as the glass tubes are very fragile and easily broken. It is desirable to place the sign behind a glass or clear plastic protective shield or to make the sign unreachable. Neon signs require transformed electrical power, and consideration also must be given to the concealment and access requirements of remotely located transformers. Painting tube standoffs, housings, and crossovers the same color as the sign background is recommended. Signs should be designed to provide the same level of lighting intensity in each sign element, and it also is desirable to minimize the number of tube crossovers.

Panel signs are constructed as a flat panel rather than as separate letters. These signs provide, in effect, both the sign letter and the background in one package. The background material and the foreground letters may be clear, translucent, or opaque. The letters may be painted, silk-screened, added as decals, or etched on the background surface, or they may be thin individual letters cut from wood, plastic, or metal and stuck to the background surface. The letters may also be cut out of the panel to form a negative image.

Panel signs may be made of any material. If illuminated, the panel is often made of plastic with letters painted on the surface or on all areas except the letters painted, to create a negative image. Light sources are located behind the panel, and this light passes through the face to reveal the letter. Sandblasting the sign letters into mirrored glass may create a similar sign. The sandblasting removes the silvering from the mirror back and permits light to pass through the now-translucent glass surface.

A sign that combines the best features of panel signs and neon signs consists of a clear plastic panel that is back painted. A computer-generated logotype is then routed into the back of this panel. Then neon is carefully shaped to align with the routed grooves.

FIGURE 4-11
*Blade signs (signs attached perpendicular to the storefront)
assist in store identification by serving custormers approaching
the store from the side.*

Non-illuminated panel signs may be affixed directly to the storefront surface, placed on pins, or hung like a picture. If the panel sign is illuminated, it is called a box sign. Box signs may be surface mounted (prohibited in most malls) or recessed. If recessed, box signs can be carefully integrated into a storefront to create a subtle and distinctive sign. Because virtually any pattern may be etched or silk-screened onto the background surface, panel signs offer the designer the greatest freedom of expression. The sign is not limited to letters but may also incorporate pictorial or abstract designs, which provide illuminated works of art as well as store identification.

In their quest to control external store signs, shopping-center developers stipulated for many years that signs be located in a fascia band above the doors and the display windows of a store. In many cases, this is a logical location for store signs: The signs are high enough to be seen from a distance; they are not obscured by shoppers standing in front of the store; they do not block the view into the store; and they are placed in an otherwise unimportant part of the storefront. To avoid monotony developers now encourage merchants to be more creative in their sign design and location. Some centers permit signs in any part of the storefront. Many shopping areas also allow, and even encourage, signs that are placed in locations other than parallel to the storefront, for example, blade and accessory signs. Blade signs, such as shown in Figure 4-11, are situated perpendicular to the storefront and are particularly useful in narrow malls, where it is difficult for the shoppers to see signs parallel to the storefront. Accessory signs include eye-level signs on storefront glass adjacent to doors, signs inlaid in floor tiling, and three-dimensional or other signs and symbols hung from the soffit above an entrance door.

Because most storefront signs are expensive, the designer should maintain an open mind about them and should work to create signs that are effective as store identification and memorable in their location, design, and construction. A successful store sign can favorably separate one storefront design from the multitude of other storefronts in a mall.

CHAPTER 5 --- LIGHTING

Lighting is the single most important part of the design of a retail store. Good lighting can enhance a product's appearance, accentuate a special display, balance the visual elements of a store, help facilitate a sale, and create the proper mood. The first objective of store lighting should be to establish the store's image. Lighting is a central design element that, in combination with the store's other design elements, conveys an image of the value of the products sold. If the store lighting imparts a look of importance to the product, it will appear valuable; if the lighting imparts a look of commonness to the product, it will seem less valuable. Even if the merchandise is exactly the same in each store, it can be perceived as having different values—discount stores illuminated with harsh, diffuse, overhead lighting—quality stores with glare-free, directional, display illumination. It is important to recognize that the store's image can in fact be determined by its lighting. Is price the most important factor? Then the lighting must make the merchandise look common. If quality, uniqueness, and style the most important factors, then the lighting must focus on the merchandise and make it look special. If properly designed, lighting can give shoppers a reason to enter a store or not, depending on their shopping goals. Budget-minded shoppers will pass by a store that looks "too expensive" even if the merchandise is reasonably priced. The store's image must be presented correctly to satisfy the customers' expectations and lighting is a significant element of that presentation.

The second objective of lighting is to attract shoppers to the store: to focus their interest on this one store as they walk along a street or mall of many stores. Well-designed lighting can attract as many customers as a "sale" sign can. Once potential customers are in the store, proper lighting will also direct them to a certain display or toward the interior of the store, thereby increasing the possibility of purchase.

The third objective of good store lighting is to provide the right sales environment for the product. In order to display the merchandise properly, lighting must attract shoppers and enhance the quality of the product, presenting in the best light its details, materials, and colors. If the customers remove the items from the display for inspection, the lighting must permit them to evaluate the items or enable the salesperson to explain their features. Often products look good under display lighting but then appear less desirable when removed from the light. Lighting must be designed to increase sales.

The last objective of lighting is to facilitate the closing of a sale. Sales and stock areas must be well lighted so that salespersons can complete the sales transaction and deliver the product.

The process of designing lighting for retail stores has three elements: identifying the task areas of the store to be illuminated, determining the lighting criteria appropriate to each task area, and selecting light sources that satisfy these criteria (Figure 5-1).

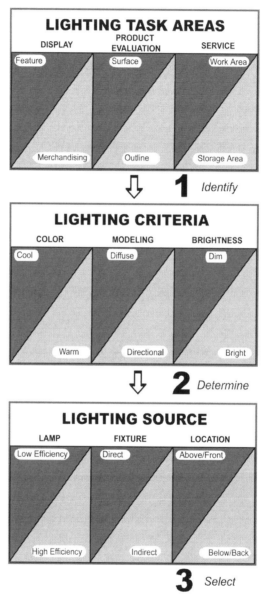

FIGURE 5-1
The three components of lighting design.

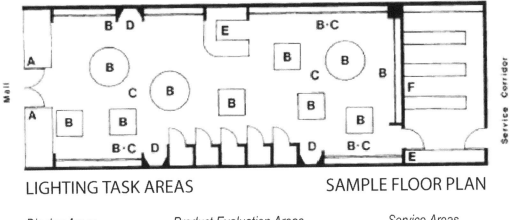

LIGHTING TASK AREAS   SAMPLE FLOOR PLAN

Display Areas	Product Evaluation Areas	Service Areas
A. Feature	C. Surface	E. Work Area
B. Merchandising	D. Outline	F. Storage Area

FIGURE 5-2
On the preliminary floor plan, the different lighting task areas should be located and identified by lighting function.

LIGHTING TASK AREAS

In any retail store, the functional operations to be illuminated can be divided into *three* lighting task areas—display, product evaluation, and service areas. The lighting requirements of each area usually differ.

After the preliminary floor plan has been developed and all the basic elements of the store design have been identified, the designer should review the plan and define each area in terms of lighting function (Figure 5-2). There often is an overlap of lighting task areas; that is, the same floor area may be used for display, product evaluation and service. The lighting, however, must be precisely designed to accommodate each movement of the product. A product on a display shelf attracts the customer, who may first gaze at it to evaluate its shape and form, then remove it for a closer examination, and then hand it to the clerk for purchase and wrapping. The shelf, the customer's hands, and the clerk's service area—each part of this sequence—must be properly analyzed and illuminated. Aisles or corridors, unless isolated or very wide, are not usually specifically illuminated but instead rely on wash light (light spilling over from other areas).

Display Areas. Display areas make the product visible to the customers. Some display areas feature products that the storeowner has selected for special

73

attention, such as a show-window display of mannequins (Figure 5-3). These areas are generally more isolated, inaccessible, and highly illuminated than are other display areas. The primary purpose of *feature* displays is to attract the customers' attention to and interest to an individual product or special group of products. The main purpose of *merchandising* displays— the other type of display area — is to attract the customers' attention to and interest in an array of products. The products in merchandise displays are usually open to inspection, on open tables or shelving, and can be handled.

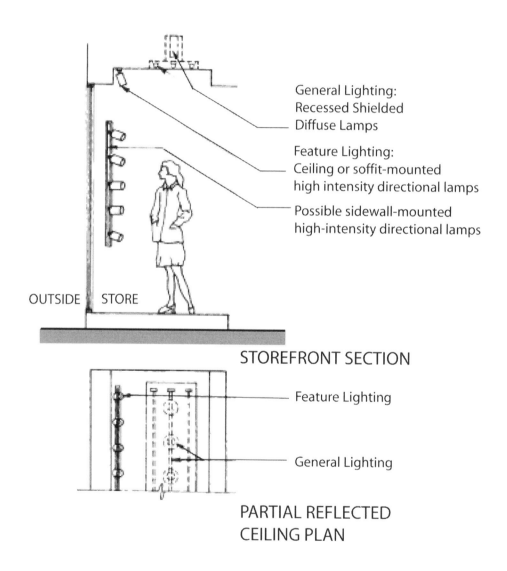

General Lighting:
Recessed Shielded
Diffuse Lamps

Feature Lighting:
Ceiling or soffit-mounted
high intensity directional lamps

Possible sidewall-mounted
high-intensity directional lamps

OUTSIDE STORE

STOREFRONT SECTION

Feature Lighting

General Lighting

PARTIAL REFLECTED
CEILING PLAN

FIGURE 5-3
A mix of diffuse and directional light sources can provide the flexibility required to properly illuminate various storefront show window displays.

Product Evaluation Areas. After customers have become interested in a product, they then *evaluate* it. This task area (product evaluation) has two subcategory possibilities that depend on the visual task: evaluations that concern the *surface* of a product and evaluations that concern the *outline* of a product. Both types may be required before customers decide to buy the product, and the evaluations may take place in two locations. For instance, an opaque vase may be displayed on a frosted glass shelf, illuminated from below against a contrasting background to demonstrate the vase's outline, proportions, and specular qualities. But the surface detail may not be clear, in which case customers may remove the vase from the shelf to examine its surface detail and color. Another light source, therefore, that reveals all surface details and color, is needed for this surface evaluation.

Clothing is often displayed on mannequins to present an overall effect and emphasize both outline and surface detail. Shoppers usually pick up clothing merchandised on racks to look at it more carefully. At this phase — either looking at a mannequin or examining clothing taken from a rack—the customers are interested in style, color, material, and labels. The lighting should assist this type of surface evaluation. After selecting an item, customers usually wish to try it on or to hold it against their body to see the fit. This viewing for fit is an outline evaluation, in which customers are concerned about shape, bulges, alignment, and the like.

The designer must determine how the customers will need to evaluate a product and where this evaluation will take place. The lighting for each task category of product evaluation, surface or outline, requires different lighting solutions. Some products, however, are not evaluated visually. Perfume, for example, may be attractively displayed in a way that may succeed in capturing the customers' interest, yet the purchase will not be completed until they test the scent. Sight plays a small part in this evaluation. Similarly, the product evaluation of a pillow or mattress depends on the sense of touch, and a gourmet food store sells its products with taste testing. Different aspects of the store design may play a stronger role than lighting does when evaluating products by senses other than sight. But lighting can still help promote sales. For example, if mattresses are being sold, the look of the product may not be as important as its touch, but the lighting can help sell the product by providing a quiet, restful environment.

Service Areas. Work areas and storage areas are the store's remaining lighting task areas. Back-room work areas may consist of alteration or tailoring spaces and wrapping, receiving, shipping, or business offices. Sales work areas include wrapping and cash counters and customer service areas. Stock and supplies may be stored in the sales area or back rooms. These areas should be evaluated to determine lighting requirements. Offices and alteration or tailoring areas need high levels of shadow-free illumination, whereas storage and receiving areas need only moderate, uniform light

LIGHTING CRITERIA

When a given area has been reviewed and designated as a specific lighting task area, the next step is to determine the appropriate lighting criteria for that area. Although there are many factors that may be considered as criteria, only those that relate to lighting sources will be discussed in this chapter. The three criteria for selecting lighting sources are the *color* of the light source, the *modeling* effect, and the *brightness* of the light source.

Color. Light sources directly affect the apparent color of displayed merchandise. This effect—the different perception of colors in different types of lighting—is called color rendering or metamerism. The designer must find the best light source to achieve the appropriate color rendering of the product displayed or activity to be illuminated.

There is no "natural" or original color for a given product, as its color seems different in natural sunlight depending on the season, time of day, geographic location, and surrounding environment and whether the sunlight is direct or indirect. Color also changes in artificial light, depending on whether the light source is incandescent, fluorescent, LED or high-intensity discharge and the various lamps available for each of these sources. Each lighting task area must be inspected to determine whether color rendering is important. Accurate color rendering is necessary when colors need to be compared, when the color of the product needs to be enhanced or grayed, when the color of an environment elsewhere needs to be simulated, or when a cool or warm store image needs to be created.

The customers' ability to compare colors may be a requirement in product-display areas but may not be an issue in service areas if workers can distinguish different colored products by other means, such as product number. In some service areas, however, correct lighting may be critical. For example, a tailor must be able to match thread color correctly with a material color in a suit of clothes. The human eye adapts to the color of a space, and so the light therein, whether warm or cold, will appear "white" in a short period of time. But abrupt color changes between spaces in a store should be avoided, as the eye adapts to the lighting of the first area and retains that state for a period of time in a new area. This could cause a salesperson coming from the back room with different color lighting and a customer viewing a display to see two different colors for the same displayed product. Certain products, such as traditional business clothing, typically muted blues and grays, require a good color-discriminating environment. Other products, such as casual clothing, may be brightly colored and easy to distinguish in any lighting.

The colors of certain products may be enhanced (intensified) or grayed (made duller looking) by using the proper light source. The spectral distribution of each light source differs, and knowing how a given source distorts the color of a product permits the designer to change its color appearance. For example, such unwrapped food items as meat, coffee beans, and bread can be color enhanced under warmer lighting, which brings out the reds, browns, and yellows. Sometimes it is desirable to gray a product's color, such as for diamonds. Diamonds must appear clear white to be most marketable, but many diamonds have a yellow cast under warm light. Therefore, diamonds should be displayed under a cool light source that has a uniform spectral distribution, including the blue bands. This tends to gray any yellow in the diamond. This practice is not deceptive if the product is presented in artificial "white" light simulating natural lighting conditions, that is, a north light, which is the jeweler's benchmark for color rendering. For feature-display lighting, in which dramatic effects are desired, colored lenses or color-variable technology can be employed in light sources to enhance a product color to an unnatural extreme. This type of lighting is like theatrical lighting, and facilities to permit color adjustment for displays are often required by merchandisers.

Sometimes, it is important to display a product under a light source that accurately reflects the lighting conditions of the environment in which the product will later be used, such as with facial cosmetics. Makeup mirrors should allow customers to adjust the lighting to reflect the various lighting conditions in which they may wear the cosmetics, such as daylight, office, and residential light. The lighting should thus offer a range of cool and warm lighting. In addition, products for use only in the home under natural, incandescent, or other warm source conditions— for example, furniture and furnishings—should be presented in neutral to warm lighting, to reduce the possibility of customers' returning products because they selected the wrong color.

Finally, the color of the light source must be considered in terms of how it will affect the store's overall mood and image. Warm lighting throughout the store in random light patterns creates an atmosphere of gaiety and intimacy, whereas general cool lighting in a higher intensity creates a feeling of somberness and detachment. The former may be appropriate in a toy store and may be the most significant color-rendering issue for that store, whereas the latter may be a major color-rendering factor for a financial institution or a store selling religious artifacts. Warm light also makes a store seem smaller and more intimate, and cool lighting enlarges the apparent size of a store.

Color temperature is a method of determining the color appearance of a light source. It is measured in degrees Kelvin. Although it permits the differentiation of color between similar light sources, it does not predict the sources' color-rendering ability. The lower (2000°K) color temperatures indicate a reddish source; the medium (3000°K) color temperatures indicate a yellow-white source; and the high (5000 °K) color temperatures indicate a bluish-white source.

To determine the color-rendering ability of a light source, one must look at its color-rendering index (CRI). CRI may be applied to various sources to determine their color-rendering ability compared with light sources of the same color temperature. The CRI theoretically ranges from 0 to 100. The higher the CRI number is, the closer the color rendition will be to the reference. For example, cool white lamps may have a Kelvin temperature of 4100, but the CRI of a standard lamp may be 60, and the CRI of an enhanced lamp might be 75. Thus the enhanced lamp is much closer in color rendition to the standard reference and should be selected if more accurate color rendering is important.

In summary, designers should select lamps that complement the store's product, from the lower, yellow-red, warmer color temperatures to the higher, blue-white, cooler color temperatures. In addition, they should choose sources that provide an adequate color rendition that relates to the lighting conditions of the product in use.

Modeling. Modeling is lighting to create a three-dimensional effect in a product display. A completely *diffuse* light source eliminates all modeling effect, or shadow, whereas an entirely *direct* light creates a severe modeling effect on a product (harsh shadow). Diffuse lighting is analogous to the flat, shadow less effect of daytime lighting in a fog—direct lighting produces the strong, delineated shadows of a single candle in a dark room.

Some retail lighting tasks require a great degree of modeling effect; others, none; and for some a combination of diffuse and direct lighting sources is the best solution. The designer must make this judgment for each lighting task area. Display lighting, for example, often requires dramatic lighting, which can be created through a modeling effect. Feature displays, too, are often dramatically illuminated to accentuate the visual features of products beyond the normal lighting range (Figure 5-4).

This is the nature of drama in display: Colors can be made more colorful,

FIGURE 5-4
High-intensity direct lighting of displays creates visual drama.

textures richer, details sharper, and features sometimes revealed to the point of visual distortion. The intent of this dramatic lighting effect is to capture the customers' attention. Even products that need not be modeled in product-evaluation areas may be modeled when in a feature display. Thus a yellow cotton towel appears significantly more interesting under a bright, direct, warm light source than under a bright, diffused, cool source. And in a properly designed display, it can become more than just a towel; it can become a work of art. Direct lighting is, therefore, useful for creating interesting, dramatic feature displays. It may also be used for merchandising displays (displays in which customers may handle the product). However, the designer must consider how the lighting will change when the product is removed from the display for examination, which may remove the magic of controlled modeling. Often, the display lights must be used in the product-evaluation area as well, to prevent a great change in the appearance of the product when it is removed from the shelf. If this is not desirable, a well lighted, nearby feature display can be maintained as a visual reference point.

Photography by Jill Greer / Greer Photo

FIGURE 5-5
The proper combination of diffuse and direct lighting provides a balanced product display with reduced shadowing.

Even if dramatic effect is not desired, displays may be modeled simply to reveal the three-dimensional nature of a product or its interesting surface. In this case, a true representation of the product is desired. To achieve this effect, the designer should use a combination of direct and diffuse lighting to create the best normal (non-dramatic) lighting conditions (Figure 5-5). This is the criterion for most store displays. The designer should strive to achieve natural but enhanced color, modeling, and brightness effects to present the product in its best light.

In product-evaluation areas, oblique shadows may be required to help the customers examine the texture or detail of a product, such as the fabric of a chair or the etching of clear glass. For other products, a three-dimensional effect is needed

---

for the customers to evaluate the outline of a sculpture, a flower, or a hat. Some products require little modeling effect for evaluation when other factors, such as color or intensity of light, are more significant. Linens, towels, carpeting, and other flat products usually fall into this category. For most work and storage areas, diffuse lighting is preferable, because the tasks to be illuminated, such as writing or using office machines would not be aided by the introduction of shadows. And where demanding tasks are performed on machines, such as a tailor working on a sewing machine, shadow-less diffuse light is essential.

Brightness. Lighting brightness can be viewed directly or indirectly. Direct or primary brightness is perceived when the viewer looks directly into the light source. Indirect or secondary brightness comes from light reflected from a surface. Because secondary brightness is the most common brightness developed by the retail store designer, we shall call it simply "brightness."

Brightness is a relative factor that depends on the following elements: the reflectivity of the object illuminated the background contrast of the object, and the intensity of the light source. Brightness can range from dim to bright as perceived by the viewer and is subject to the preceding three elements of lighting. The designer must decide on the brightness level needed for each lighting task, within the range of dim to bright. Which areas of a retail store should appear bright to the shoppers as they look around the store? In most cases, of the three lighting task areas—display, product evaluation, and service —the display areas should be the brightest, as the first objective of display is to focus the customers' attention on the merchandise. This approach to creating pools of brightness on displays is appropriate when merchandise attraction is the primary goal of lighting and the unique nature of the merchandise is the primary image of the store. If the store is selling price before uniqueness, however, the objective of lighting may be to provide a more uniform level of brightness, equally emphasizing the merchandise, product evaluation, and service.

Each product to be illuminated has a certain reflectance, which depends on the product's color. White products reflect over 80 percent of the light illuminating them, whereas green or brown objects may reflect only 20 percent of the light. Photometric brightness —the degree of light intensity — can be measured with a photometer; the reflectance of the product affects the level of brightness measured. Brightness measured from a reflecting surface is expressed in foot-lamberts, which may be estimated by multiplying the object's reflectance factor (the factor can be obtained from the photometric reading) by the number of foot-candles produced by the light source.

The quantity of light emitted from a light source is measured in lumens. For example, a typical cool white, 32-watt fluorescent lamp has a normal output of 2,800 lumens. The density of light in a given area is measured in foot-candles, which are determined by averaging the total lumens emitted over the area illuminated.

In other words, the brightness of a display is how much light is delivered to the display (foot-candles) and how much is reflected back to the customer (foot lamberts). Because light-colored objects have a greater reflectance factor, they always appear brighter than dark-colored objects do in the same light source with the same background. The designer should gauge the general color reflectance of the merchandise to be displayed and note these percentages of reflectivity on the design plan. If the designer does not have a photometer, known reflective samples can be used to estimate an item's reflectance factor. Similarly, instead of trying to determine foot-candles, the designer can consult a lighting consultant or engineer who can estimate them accurately.

Products may also have a specular or mirror like quality. Light reflectance caused by a product's specular quality may either enhance or detract from the product. Enhancing reflections give a product sparkle and glitter and can be seen in glass, silver, jewelry, and similar products. Detracting reflections, known as veiling reflections, are caused by reflections in packaging materials and glass surfaces in front of products such as countertops and show windows. These reflections obscure a product's detail. To eliminate undesirable reflections, the designer must position the light source so that it will not be reflected in the product displayed. Usually, this means locating the light source above or behind the customer. Where desirable, to increase reflections, the opposite approach should be followed.

The second factor of brightness is background contrast. Background contrast (brightness ratio) is important to establishing the proper conditions for product evaluation. As we noted, there are two categories of product evaluation: review of the product surface and review of the product outline. If the product surface must be examined, the contrast between the product and background should be minimized, and the ratio of the reflectance of the product to the background should be less than 1:3. If the ratio is higher, the eye will adjust to the brighter background, which will obscure the details of the product.

If the product's outline is more important than its surface detail, the ratio of brightness can be increased, thereby revealing less detail but emphasizing the shape or form. In this case, a light-colored product would be displayed against a dark background, and vice versa. The wrong background material can result in reflected glare, which is the reflection of light sources by a background. Background materials, therefore, should have a matte finish, no matter what its reflectance may be. Reflected glare impairs the customers' ability to see surface details or a product's outline.

The final factor of brightness is the light source, which affects brightness by its lumen output and concentration. Some light sources, such as reflector bulbs, are designed to concentrate light, whereas others, such as fluorescent tubes, do not. Light sources vary in their lumen output. The designer must figure the number of foot-candles needed for a given task area, taking into account many factors, such as the reflectance of the product, the background of the product, and the brightness of all other areas inside or outside the store in relation to the task area.

Appropriate levels of store illumination depend on many factors. Usually the store requires a reference level of ambient light that is sufficient to illuminate generally the store's circulation paths. This ambient light level may be provided by fluorescent or other diffuse lighting or may simply be the result of "wash light" from accent lighting. In either case the designer must use contrasting lighting for the products for sale and the other areas of the store such as the corridors or service counters.

The amount of contrast between one area of a store illumination and another is known as a contrast ratio. The designer should bear in mind the following general guidelines for a contrast ratio:

1. Feature displays should have brightness five times that of other nearby surfaces.

2. If a noticeable transition from one area to another (such as merchandising areas and circulation areas) is desirable, one space should be three times brighter than the other.

3. If lighting continuity is required, a ratio of less than 2:1 should be maintained.

4. Color discrimination is lost at levels below 10 foot-lamberts

Finally, the designer must recognize the relationship of the lighting levels of the store to the mall or street outside and, if possible, create a positive contrast ratio to the illumination of these adjacent public spaces.

LIGHTING SOURCES

The following discussion will be restricted to artificial, non-decorative light sources. Retail stores are similar to legitimate theaters in their lighting needs: both require precise lighting control in order to dramatize the environment. This control is most easily attained by excluding natural light, rather than by attempting to modulate it. Although sometimes natural light may be necessary, for reasons such as energy efficiency or psychology, the techniques of controlling sunlight to achieve the best possible lighting of each task area during the day and evening are beyond the scope of this book.

Once the designer has identified the lighting task areas in the store and established the lighting criteria for each, the lighting source for each area must be selected according to these criteria. Each lighting source has three components: the lamp, the fixture, and the location of the source in relation to the task. Each component has an effect on the color rendering, modeling, and brightness of the area to be illuminated.

For example, if the task area is a business suit display, the designer may have lighting criteria calling for accurate, blue-spectrum color rendering; diffuse lighting of the suit surface; and moderate brightness without glare. The lighting source selected might then be an enhanced cool white fluorescent lamp with a single lamp and a metal tube fixture, to be located in front of the suits. By knowing the various properties of each lighting source, the correct lighting can be chosen.

Lamps.

Filament Lamps (low efficiency). An incandescent lamp consists of a wire filament sealed in a glass bulb containing an inert gas. When an electrical current is passed through the wire, it heats to the point of incandescence and emits light. The lamp (or bulb) should not be confused with the fixture that houses it.

All incandescent lamps have similar color-rendering properties. They emit a warm, yellow-white light that is very flattering to human skin color, is bright and cheerful, and enhances the red— yellow range of colors. It is, however, a very poor light in which to discriminate blues, blacks, and greens—these colors tend to gray. Tungsten and halogen gas incandescent lamps provide a more balanced color rendering than do typical argon and nitrogen gas incandescent sources.

Incandescent lamps used in retail stores to illuminate a task (as opposed to decoration) fall into two modeling categories: diffuse or directional (Figure 5-6). Diffuse incandescent lamps are either A-bulbs (arbitrary shape) or P-bulbs (pear shape). These bulbs are housed in fixtures that reflect their light either directionally or diffusely. A- and P-bulbs are inexpensive to replace, have a rated life of about one thousand hours, and are filled with argon and nitrogen. In addition to A- and P-bulbs, directional incandescent lamps include R-bulbs (reflector), PAR-bulbs (parabolic aluminized reflector), and MR-bulbs (multifaceted open reflector). R- and PAR-bulbs are filled with argon and nitrogen; PAR-bulbs may also contain tungsten filaments and halogen gas lamps. MR-bulbs are exclusively tungsten filament, halogen gas lamps. These three bulb types (MR, R, and PAR) have built-in reflectors that direct light and do not require reflectors in the fixture housing. The interiors of R. and PAR-bulbs are silvered to create this reflector, whereas an

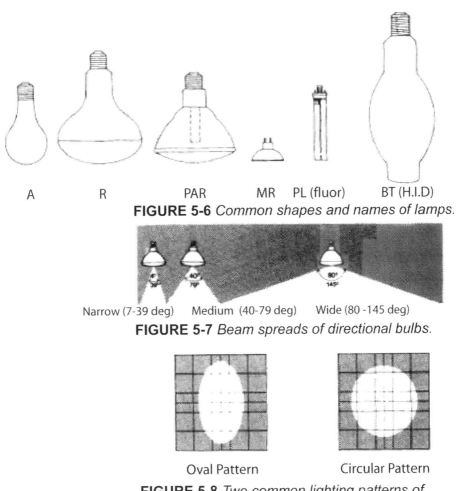

FIGURE 5-6 *Common shapes and names of lamps.*

Narrow (7-39 deg)   Medium (40-79 deg)   Wide (80 -145 deg)

FIGURE 5-7 *Beam spreads of directional bulbs.*

Oval Pattern   Circular Pattern

FIGURE 5-8 *Two common lighting patterns of directional bulbs. The oval pattern may be useful for the lighting of rectangular surfaces.*

MR-bulb consists of a tungsten filament, halogen gas lamp that operates at low voltage and is attached to a small, mirrored reflector. MR bulbs may require a transformer to reduce voltage for their operation or may operate at line voltage. R-, PAR-, and MR-bulbs are more expensive to replace than are A- or P-bulbs. R-, PAR-, and MR-bulbs all have an average rated life of about 2,000 hours.

Beam spread is the shape and size of the light emitted by a lamp. Directional bulbs are available in various beam spreads, including WFL (wide flood), FL (flood), MFL (medium flood), SP (spot), NSP (narrow spot), and VNSP (very narrow spot).These spreads may range from 7 to 145 degrees, depending on the type of bulb, and they may have a circular or an oval configuration (Figure 5-7 and 5-8).

Incandescent lamps produce 17 to 22 lumens per watt, whereas fluorescent lamps produce 58 to 100 lumens per watt, metal halide high-intensity discharge (HID) produce 80 to 125 lumens per watt, and light-emitting diode fixtures (LED) can produce in excess of 135 lumens per watt. Although incandescent lamps are less efficient than fluorescent and other lamps are (the more lumens there are per watt, the greater the efficiency will be), directional incandescent lamps provide a wide variety of options to illuminate display areas effectively and precisely, in a manner still unmatched by most discharge or LED lamps. In addition,

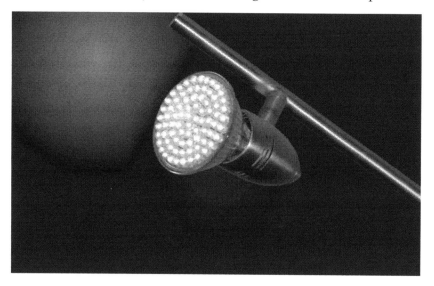

A   LED directional bulb in a track lighting fixture.

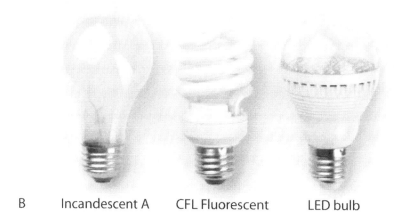

B   Incandescent A   CFL Fluorescent   LED bulb

FIGURE 5-9
Different lamp types can be used in the same socket with similar lighting effects, but with a considerable difference in energy consumption.

incandescent lamps are available in a wide range of brightness and can be dimmed (with dimmer controls) at a reasonable expense. Therefore, when the lighting criteria for a task area call for warm color rendering and/or a precise directional modeling effect, incandescent lamps have been the lamps to be used. These features also are now available in some discharge lamps and LED lamps and this is an area of constant improvement, updating and changes in product availability (Figures 5-9 A & B).

Discharge Lamps-Fluorescent (medium efficiency). There are two types of discharge lamps, fluorescent and high-intensity discharge (HID).

Fluorescent lamps are glass tubes coated on the inside with phosphor and filled with a low-pressure, inert gas and a small amount of mercury vapor. Inside each end of the tube are electrodes that act as terminals for an electric arc, which excites the atoms of mercury vapor to release ultraviolet radiation, which in turn activates the phosphor and emits visible light. These lamps are relatively inexpensive to replace and are rated for a life of approximately 9,000 to 20,000 hours. Fluorescent lamps require an electrical ballast to control the electrical current to the lamp; each fixture and some lamps come equipped with the necessary ballast.

Fluorescent lamps are generally non-directional, diffuse lighting sources and provide little modeling effect. With regard to brightness, fluorescent lamps are efficient light sources, using up to 80 percent less energy than incandescent sources do. They can be used with incandescent lights to achieve a balance of diffuse and directional light. One advantage to using fluorescent lamps is that they increase lighting levels without becoming as hot as incandescent lights do. They illuminate large areas efficiently and have very long rated lives compared with incandescent lamps. They can be dimmed, but the required dimmer systems are more expensive than for incandescent. Fluorescent lamps are now available in many different shapes. The standard is the straight tube. Also common is the U bent tube used in a 2-foot-square fixture. Other useful shapes are the PL-lamp which is a short double or quadruple tube that can be placed in recessed reflector direct lighting fixtures to produce the look and lighting performance of an incandescent A-lamp but has a much longer life and greater efficiency (75 percent energy savings and up to ten times the life of incandescent lights). Compact fluorescent lamps (CFL) have a spiral configuration, are self-ballasted and may be used to replace incandescent A lamps with a considerable reduction in wattage. Fluorescent lamps, which are modeled after the R (reflector) series incandescent floodlighting bulbs, are also available with similar efficiency and lamp life.

Fluorescent lamps offer a wide range of color rendering. Enhanced fluorescent lamps are available which have a broad spectrum of light that is balanced to provide excellent color rendering. These lamps are recommended for use in retail stores, although the lumen output of these lamps will be somewhat less than that of the standard lamps. The trichomatic series of lamps was developed specifically to provide excellent color rendering, by emitting narrow spectral bands of color, as opposed to the broad spectrum of standard fluorescent lamps, without diminishing the lumen output. The CRI for such lamps ranges from 70 to 85. The lamps with a higher CRI and greater lumen output are more expensive at initial purchase (but can offer an overall savings by reducing the total number of fixtures required for a store. The cost of lamps becomes significant when designing a large retail store with many fixtures.

Discharge Lamps-H.I.D. Lamps (high efficiency). High-intensity discharge (HID) lamps are similar to fluorescent lamps in operation and efficiency and to incandescent lamps in shape and size. The gas vapor is mercury, metal halide with mercury, or high-pressure sodium. These lamps have a rated life of 5,000 to 20,000 hours, and like fluorescent lamps, they also require a ballast to control the electrical current to the lamp. Color-corrected metal halide 3000°K color-temperature lamps do not have the smooth spectral distribution of an incandescent or deluxe fluorescent lamp and, therefore, are less able to provide accurate color rendering. But they can be an effective substitute for fluorescent lamps and for some flood lamp incandescent applications. Uncorrected metal halide lamps tend to gray reds and enhance blues, greens, and yellows. Color-corrected high-pressure sodium lamps are also available that have been specifically designed for retail use (CR1 80).

HID lamps can be used for general diffuse illumination. In open-reflector fixtures, these lamps can give some of the appearance and modeling effect of incandescent lighting. In regard to brightness, metal halide lamps are even more efficient (80 to 125 lumens per watt) than fluorescent lamps. They may be used if the cost of lighting operation and low maintenance are important. They can be dimmed, but the dimmers for fluorescent lamps are more expensive than those for incandescent systems. In addition, HID fixtures require a warm-up period of several minutes before they reach their full lighting intensity. Colors may shift in a HID, and therefore, the designer should use the same wattage, manufacturer, and type of lamp in a single store.

LED Lamps (high efficiency). Light-emitting diode (LED) lights are semi-conduction light sources, very efficient, and are a type of solid-state lighting. In the past, they were typically used for indicator and specialty lights, but now there are types of LED fixtures available for retail lighting use. These fixtures will include floodlights, spotlights, tube (to replace the use of fluorescent) and strip lights. They have a very long lamp life (in excess of 25,000 hours), are efficient, shock-resistant, dimmable, and have minimal heat generation. Improvements in LED lighting are developing rapidly making this source more feasible for use in retail stores. Color rendering, which had been an issue, previously, has been improved considerably. Given that code energy requirements are making the task of a lighting designer more challenging, the option to utilize LED fixtures to reduce energy use can give the designer more flexibility to achieve a successful lighting solution that is energy efficient and effective. Large stores that would, in the past, use fluorescent tube general lighting can use LED fixtures to achieve a similar lighting effect. If the store will have long hours of operation and has a long-term lease (say ten years or more), the use of LED lights can reduce costs of energy and maintenance resulting in considerable savings and a smaller "carbon footprint".

Fixtures. The following are desirable performance characteristics of light fixtures used in retail stores: easy adjustment, reduced heat output, durable sockets, easy re-lamping, long life, excellent color rendering, low operating cost and energy efficiency. Obviously no one fixture can satisfy all these general performance characteristics and the specific requirements of modeling and brightness. The task of the designer is to consider the options and decide on the best, overall, system of lighting.

Two types of light fixtures are used in retail stores: direct and indirect. Direct lighting fixtures aim the light directly on the task, whereas indirect lighting fixtures direct the light toward the ceiling or soffit above, either of which then reflects this light down to the task below. Direct lighting can be either diffuse or directional; indirect lighting is invariably diffuse.

Direct Lighting. The following direct lighting fixtures are categorized by fixtures that permit the fixtures installation of more than one type of lamp: recessed, open reflector, non-reflector, and adjustable down lights; wall washers; track lighting; troffers; and pendant and surface-mounted fixtures.

Recessed down lights are installed above the ceiling with only a small trim ring left exposed below the ceiling. They are manufactured for general-service (A and P-bulbs), reflector incandescent, and HID lamps. Almost all the light open reflector down lights are the least complicated of the down lights. They consist of a simple metal fixture with a socket that houses a general-service lamp or HID lamp (for HID fixtures, a ballast is also provided) and a dome-shaped reflector to redirect the light from the lamp. A common reflector for this type is a specular Alzak, a highly polished, dome-shaped reflector that is available in a clear or gold finish. Open reflectors provide excellent general lighting with some modeling effect. They offer easy lamp maintenance (no parts need be removed to get to the lamp and in some cases it can be removed with an extension pole) and reasonable direct glare control. For further glare control, open reflector down-lights are available with different low-brightness trim rings that extend up into the fixture. These trim rings may be grooved or have a non-reflective finish. In either case, the direct glare is eliminated for normal viewing angles.

Non-reflector down lights use a fully recessed metal housing with a socket to receive a lamp. A transformer is also provided if the down light uses low-voltage MR-bulbs. The lamp must have its own reflector system, as none is provided in the fixture itself. Therefore, non-reflector down-lights are designed to house R-, PAR-, or MR-bulbs, all of which have built-in reflector systems. These fixtures may also use low-brightness grooved or non-reflective baffles mounted between the lamp and the bottom of the fixture. Non-reflector down light fixtures offer directional light as well as a great degree of modeling effect, depending on the lamp used. The lamps are relatively more expensive (compared with lamps not having reflector systems) and are more difficult to maintain (the lamps cannot be easily removed with poles), but there is the advantage of having a new optical system installed with each replacement.

Adjustable down lights consist of a metal housing that is either fully recessed into the ceiling (open adjustable type) or semi recessed (the "eyeball" type). Each type has an adjustable socket and uses lamps with internal reflector systems: R-, PR-, or MR-bulbs. These light sources provide unobtrusive, glare-free, directional light and can be adjusted to illuminate objects that are not located directly below the fixture — the lamp can be rotated almost 360 degrees and can tilt up to 35 degrees. These fixtures have the same maintenance qualities, as do non-reflector down lights; that is, the lamps are expensive and difficult to replace.

Wall washers consist of a fully recessed metal housing that has a fixed socket with or without a built-in reflector. Therefore, they can house both reflector and non-reflector lamps. They are designed to be located in a series along, and about 3 feet away from, the wall and one another. When properly installed, they cast even, diffuse illumination on the wall; they do not direct light onto horizontal surfaces below except by reflectance.

Track lighting is derived from theater lighting and is a system of direct lighting fixtures that are fully exposed and fully adjustable and may be relocated anywhere along the track—a continuous linear electrical power source and hanging system. Track lighting fixtures use reflector lamps and R-, PAR-, or MR bulbs, and MR track lights also have integral solid-state transformers. A wide variety of fixture housings are available to the designer with most varying simply in style, color, and material.

Track lighting offers a great degree of flexibility to the designer, because not only the direction of the light, but also its location can be changed. This feature makes track lighting an ideal auxiliary or primary lighting source for a retail store. Track lights are also available with colored filters that attach directly to the fixture. The biggest drawback to track lights is the potential direct-glare problem. Because the lights can be positioned in any direction, it is likely the light source will be visible and produce glare. Some baffles are available to control glare, which cause the lamp to be recessed deep into the fixture. Even though this effectively cuts off light, store personnel must be instructed to be aware of the problem of direct glare, and the fixtures must always be positioned to control this problem.

Troffers are metal boxes that can be fully recessed into the ceiling. They are square or rectangular, house and connect ballasts and one to four fluorescent tubes, and have a lens through which the light passes. Troffers are an economical means of providing general diffuse illumination. The biggest problem associated with them is glare. Although the lamps are concealed, the lens at the ceiling plan becomes a source of glare and tends to draw the customer's eyes up, away from the merchandise. Special lenses, like parabolic section louvers, are available to control this surface brightness. These louvers are of the egg-crate type, with cells varying in size to as small as an inch square. They have special optical properties to reduce wasted light and direct it downward, resulting in a fixture that appears dark when the lamps are lit. These lenses are more expensive than are other typical acrylic, prismatic lenses, but they eliminate the direct-glare problem. In general, the larger the cell opening is, the greater the light output of the louver will be. Pendant and surface-mounted fixtures have fully exposed and finished housings. Pendants are suspended from the ceiling on rods and are used where ceilings are high, requiring fixtures to be lower, or where ceilings are unfinished. Surface-mounted fixtures are attached directly to a ceiling or soffit and are exposed to view. These fixtures may be used on unfinished ceilings or as an architectural feature. Pendant and surface-mounted fixtures have design and optical qualities similar to those of the direct lighting, recessed, and track light fixtures discussed earlier.

Indirect Lighting. Indirect lighting is used to achieve general diffuse illumination. The light is directed toward the ceiling and reflected onto the task area below: The lighting effect is uniform and diffuse. Indirect lighting is often used with directional lighting sources because it is totally diffuse and provides no modeling effect. The color rendering of the fixture depends on both the lamp used and the color of the ceiling surface that reflects the light. Care must be taken not to attempt intense lighting levels, or extreme ceiling brightness will result, detracting from the merchandise. Indirect pendant fixtures are fully exposed, and finished fixtures are suspended 18 to 36 inches below and directed up toward a ceiling.

These may use incandescent, fluorescent, LED or HID lamps.

Cove and bracket fixtures and sconces are wall mounted 18 to 36 inches below a ceiling. They may use fluorescent or incandescent lamps. Cove fixtures provide indirect light and are suitable for general illumination. They are composed of fixtures hidden behind a cove molding or a decorative linear box. Brackets and sconces are individual fixtures mounted onto walls. They can provide either directed or indirect light and are usually used for decorative purposes. Floor or

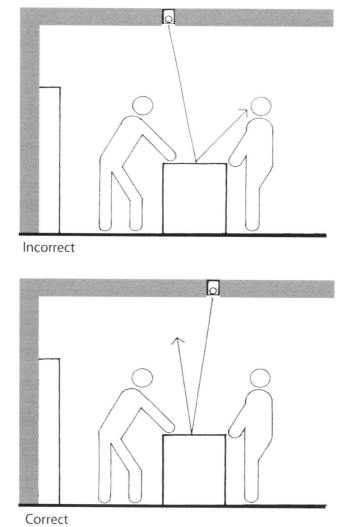

Incorrect

Correct

FIGURE 5-10
Light sources should be located above and in front to minimize veiling reflections and glare.

store fixture—mounted light fixtures may use fluorescent, incandescent, or HID lamps. These are typically used with low ceilings, which do not permit the use of pendant fixtures.

Location. In most cases, lighting sources for product displays should be located in front of and above the product to be illuminated. There are two reasons for this positioning: It creates a natural lighting effect similar to daylight, and it minimizes direct glare from the fixture, as it is aimed away from the viewer.

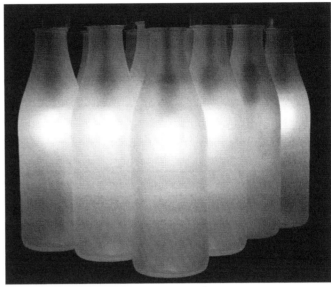

FIGURE 5-11
Glass art may be effectively displayed using light from behind.

FIGURE 5-12
This store uses a combination of light wash behind the product and direct light onto the product.

Because the light reflected from a horizontal case bounces up and away from the viewer, veiling reflections are also minimized (Figure 5-10). For similar reasons, this position is also frequently used for product-evaluation and service areas. Sometimes, however, it may be desirable to illuminate a displayed product from below or even behind, as this may make it appear more interesting or sculptured. Clear vases and glass art, for example, transmit light from below and thereby appear luminous (Figure 5-11). Light from below or behind can also make products appear more dramatic or unusual simply because they are rarely displayed in that manner. Light can be used to wash the surface behind a product, thereby silhouetting the product's outline (Figure 5-12). This type of lighting placement can be used with a directional light source in front of and above the product, to show its surface details as well as its outline. If a product's outline is the key to its sale and the surface is less important, back lighting can be used alone.

Other factors of source location include the relationship of one source to another for the creation of uniform lighting distribution, and the number of sources required to achieve a certain lighting brightness. It is beyond the scope of this text to discuss in detail the characteristics of each manufacturer's lighting fixtures, or the method of spacing fixtures for uniform illumination or for a desired lighting brightness level. The designer should obtain such information from a lighting manufacturer or consultant.

EXIT LIGHTING

In most jurisdictions, exit lighting must have emergency standby power from a generator, or it must have a battery backup source. The designer should review selection options with the local code authority.

The typical fixture used for emergency or exit sign lighting is a self-contained battery pack, with lamps. It may be either surface or recessed mounted. Recessed units are recommended, as they can be made to fit into the store design. These units are generally required by code to be installed to provide a source of path, corridor, and stair exit illumination inside the store in the event of a power failure. The other fixtures should be located along the exit path to provide the required code illumination.

*   *   *

Thanks for reading:
STORE DESIGN: A Complete Guide to Designing Successful Retail Stores.

Did you like the book? Your reviews and recommendations are always welcome ... *W. Green*

Visit my author page at www.WGreen.me

CHECKLIST FOR STORE DESIGN

Store Name: _____

    Location: _____

    Size: _____

A. General

1. What is the store's construction budget?

2. What is the schedule for the store's opening?

3. Have the base drawings and lease documents from the landlord been received?

4. Has a builder been selected?

5. Who will represent the store owner when making design decisions?

B. Image

1. How will your customers be drawn to the store?

    a. They will be directed to the store by advertising or other promotion.

    b. They will be attracted to the store as they pass by.

2. How will your customers select the products?

a. Most products will be displayed openly. Adequate product-evaluation information will be located at the sales point.

b. Most products will be in closed displays, and sales personnel will be available to provide product-evaluation information.

3. What is the image of the store?

a. Exclusive or popular.

b. Traditional or avant-garde.

c. Popular priced or expensive.

d. Serious or playful.

e. Service oriented or self-service.

f. Quiet or noisy.

g. Subdued or spirited.

h. Cool or warm.

4. What is the market for the store's products?

a. Young, middle-aged, older.

b. Men, women, boys, girls.

c. Below-average, average, or above-average income level.

5. Are there any other stores that you find attractive and relevant to the design of this store?

C. Spatial Organization

1. How will the circulation paths be designed?

   a. On one level or many levels?

   b. Can a shopper evaluate products from a circulation area, or is the circulation space solely to permit movement from one area to another?

2. What is the best location for the cash counter?

   a. In the front, middle, or rear of the store?

3. Can products be displayed in or on the cash counter?

4. Will the wrapping counter be separate from the cash counter?

5. What percentage of the store should be devoted to storage? Which items will be stored?

6. Is a public washroom desirable or required? Are separate employee washrooms desirable or required? (Check local codes)

7. Should employee kitchen, dining, or locker facilities be provided?

8. Is special equipment required for repair or production? If so, what are its spatial and mechanical/electrical requirements?

9. How many employees will work in the store at any one time? What will their roles be?

10. How and where will sales be transacted?

11. How and where will money be stored?

12. Will the store deliver products?

13. How will store deliveries be made?

14. Will any offices be required?

D. Product Display

1. Which items will be displayed?

   a. By group, such as men's suits, men's shoes, or women's shoes.

   b. By type of purchase, such as staples, convenience, and impulse items.

2. What percentage of total display area will each product require?

3. What are the qualities of each product to be displayed?

   a. Size: large/small.

   b. Class: unique/common.

   c. Price: expensive/inexpensive.

4. What display techniques will be used for each product?

   a. Presentation: massed/individual.

   b. Support: from above/from below.

   c. Integration: isolated/contextual.

5. Which products will require special displays or display techniques?

6. How will the customers evaluate each product?

   a. They will examine its surface qualities — color, texture, and so on.

   b. They will examine its shape or outline.

   c. Salesperson will be present to assist in the evaluation.

   d. Written product-evaluation material will be present at the display.

E. Storefronts (verify landlord requirements)

   1. How will the storefront be designed?

      a. Transparency: open/closed.

      b. Plan: recessed/projected.

      c. Design statement: strong/neutral.

   2. Will specific products be displayed in show windows? Or will the entire store be visible through the storefront show windows?

   3. If show windows will be used to display merchandise, will they be backed or non-backed?

   4. Will the customers be required to open a door to enter the store, or will they simply pass through an opening?

   5. Has a store logo been developed as the basis for a store sign?

F. Materials

1. What are the preferred materials for the store?

   a. Walls.

   b. Floors.

   c. Ceilings.

   d. Storefront.

   e. Fixtures and furniture.

G. Systems

1. Is a specific lighting source preferred?

   a. Incandescent.

   b. Fluorescent.

   c. HID

   d. LED

2. Are any types of light fixtures undesirable?

   a. Recessed cans.

   b. Exposed lighting, such as neon, cold cathode, or incandescent.

   c. Track lights.

   d. Surface-mounted fixtures.

   e. Troffers

f. Ambient up lighting.

3. What are the security requirements for merchandise, money, and employees?

　　a. Cameras.

　　b. Monitoring devices.

　　c. Panic buttons.

　　d. Safes or strongboxes. (Need floor structural analysis?)

　　e. Security patrol.

4. Are there special requirements for cooling or heating any areas of the store?

5. Are any products, people, or equipment susceptible to damage from excess heat, cold, moisture, dryness, light, noise, or air flow?

6. Will the store have a sound system?

7. Will the store employ a subliminal smell system?

8. Where will telephones be required?

9. Where will electrical outlets be required?

　　a. Are special isolated or dedicated outlets required for computer equipment or cash registers?

10. Is a water source required for any location?

GLOSSARY

Aluminum storefront sections: Aluminum that has been extruded to form hollow, rectangular sections used as mullions and muntins in storefront construction.

Bay window: Window(s) projecting outward from a wall.

Bi-parting door: A double door with two leaves slide away from each other in the same plane and meet at the center line of the door.

Coffer: A deeply recessed ceiling panel.

Corner store: A store located at the outside corner intersection of two malls or streets.

Demising wall: A wall that separates one tenant from another or one tenant from a common area, such as a service corridor in a shopping center.

Direct glare: Glare resulting from inadequate shielded light sources in the field of view.

Electrical ballasts: In discharge-type light fixtures, ballast supplies the high voltage to start the arc and then limits the current in the arc.

Emergency egress: The path leading to a fire exit or fire-protected exit corridor.

Enclosed mall: A shopping center building having a centrally heated and air conditioned enclosed public circulation space that serves to connect all the stores.

Fascia: A horizontal band above the storefront doors and windows, on which a store sign may often be placed.

Feather edge: An undesirable millwork condition in which the wood is milled to produce a finely tapered and easily broken edge.

Flame spread rating: A numerical designation (from 0 to 100) indicating the resistance of a building material to flaming combustion over its surface. A noncombustible material has a rating of 0.

Foot-candle: The unit used to measure the amount of light that reaches a surface. Foot-candles equal lumens divided by the area illuminated in square feet.

Foot-lambert: A unit of brightness equal to the emission from a light source or the surface reflection of one lumen per square foot of area illuminated.

Free-standing store: A shop or department store located on a site that is attached to no other building and that may have adjacent parking on all sides.

Furring strips: Continuous metal channels that are attached parallel to walls at regularly spaced intervals and to which drywall is screwed in wall construction.

Glazing: Installing glass in windows, doors, or storefronts.

Gold leaf: Very thin sheets of rolled gold used in gilding or inscribing glass, as for signs.

Gross leasable area (GLA): The total leasable area of a store, usually the actual store area between the demising walls and the lease line at the storefront.

Gypsum board: A wallboard with a paper finish and a core of gypsum plaster.

In-line store: A store located between two other stores in a shopping center or on a street.

Life style center: An open-air shopping center having upscale shops, "traditional" street-like circulation and configurations, and a proximity to affluent neighborhoods.

Lowest qualified bid: The lowest price to complete the proposed construction submitted by a bidder deemed qualified to perform the work satisfactorily.

Lumen: A unit of luminous flux or quantity of light.

Mullions: Vertical members that separate and support windows, doors, or panels set in a series.

Muntins: Horizontal members that separate and support windows, doors, or panels.

National tenant: A merchant who operates a chain of stores on a nationwide basis.

Noise reduction coefficient (NRC): The average amount of sound energy absorbed by a material over a range of frequencies between 250 Hz and 2,000 Hz.

Open mall: A shopping center composed of separate buildings arranged to form a central outdoor circulation space connecting all the stores.

Photometric brightness: The amount of foot-lamberts emitted or reflected from a light source or surface.

Pin mounting: A method of sign attachment in which the sign letters are pinned away from the sign background.

Plenum: The space between a ceiling and the floor or roof above, sometimes used as an air duct.

Program: A written compilation of all project functions, their relationships, and their space requirements.

Prototype store: A model chain store designed and constructed for the purpose of study, evaluation, and modification, leading to a program of rollout stores.

Rail: A horizontal piece in a door or window.

Rollout stores: The refinement of a store design based on prototype stores and built in many locations.

Rough-in: The completed construction process before the finishing work.

Sales volume: The gross dollar amount of retail sales for a store in a given period, usually expressed as a factor of total store area.

Scribe: A reducible wood trim that permits the carpenter to form-fit a cabinet to irregular wall surfaces.

Silicone: A sealant used to hold glass in a frame or to seal the joint between two glass panels.

Smoke density factor: A numerical designation (from 0 to 100) of a building material, indicating its surface burning characteristics and how much smoke it produces. A non-combustible material has a rating of 0.

Soffit: The exposed undersurface of any overhead component of a building, such as an arch, beam, or cornice.

Sound batting: Insulation installed in a wall to absorb sound.

Sound reverberation: The persistent echoing of previously generated sound, caused by the reflection of acoustic waves from the surfaces of enclosed spaces.

Specifications: A part of the contract documents. Specifications are in written form and detail the items of construction to be purchased and the methods of installation.

Spectral distribution: The separation of the component colors of light plotted to indicate the relative amounts of wavelength energy.

Sprinkler test drain: A point in the fire protection sprinkler line that permits local drainage of the piping after pressure testing.

Strip center: A shopping center with buildings sited to permit parking directly adjacent to shops and views of individual shops from adjacent roadways.

Stub-in: A utility duct (such as water, sewer, sprinkler, or electric) connecting a main source to a point inside the tenant's premises.

UL rating: Underwriters Laboratories (UL) is an independent organization that tests materials and equipment for fire and shock hazards and establishes and maintains standards. UL reviews and tests building components and provides a fire-resistance rating, stated in hours of fire resistance.

REFERENCES AND SUGGESTED READINGS

AWI, AWMAC and WI; 2009 *Architectural Woodwork Standards* 1st edition

Barr, Vilma, and Charles E. Broudy; 1990 *Designing to Sell*. McGraw-Hill 2 Sub edition

Cialdini, Robert B.; 1984 *Influence: How and Why People Agree on Things*. New York: Morrow.

Edwards, Betty. 1986. *Drawing on the Artist Within*. New York: Fireside.

Eysenck, Hans J. and Michael Eysenck. 1995 *Mindwatching: Why People Behave the Way They Do*. Prion.

Hopkins, Tom. 2005 *How to Master the Art of Selling*. Business Plus: Revised Updated edition

Howard, Brian; Brinsky William J. and Leitman, Seth. 2010. *Green Lighting*. McGraw Hill.

Langer, Ellen J. 1989. *Mindfulness*. Reading, MA: Addison-Wesley.

Lighting Research Center; March 2010 "Guide to Light and Color in Retail Merchandising"; Volume 8, Issue 1

Lopez, Michael J. 1995 *Retail Store Planning & Design Manual*. John Wiley & Sons Inc; 2 Sub edition

Binkley, Christina. 2010. "How Stores Lead You to Spend." Wall Street Journal. Dec. 2, pp. D1

Morgan, Tony. 2008. *Visual Merchandising: Windows and In-Store Displays for Retail*. Laurence King Publishers

Nuckolls, James L. 1983. *Interior Lighting for Environmental Designers*. New York: Wiley.

Peglar, Martin M., ed., 2008. *Stores of the Year*. Vol. 16; Visual Reference Publications

Retail Design Institute; 2009 *Stores and Retail Spaces 10*; ST Media Group International Inc.

Settle, Robert B., and Pamela L. Alreck. 1989. *Why They Buy*. New York: Wiley

Underhill, Paco. 2008. *Why We Buy*. Simon & Schuster Updated Revised Ed.

INDEX

ABOUT THE AUTHOR

William R. Green is a registered architect who has practiced architecture as a principal for several large design firms in the Chicago area. Having also worked for a pioneering regional shopping center firm as a development manager, he has experienced retail from the real estate developer perspective, as well as the viewpoint of a retail designer. Over his career he has designed many retail establishments of all types and sizes for local and national tenants.

PHOTO CREDITS

Made in the USA
Middletown, DE
26 October 2015